QUEEN MARGHERITA OF ITALY

OUT OF MY COFFIN

AN AUTOBIOGRAPHY

By

MARCHESA STELLA VITELLESCHI

(STELLA RHO)

With a Foreword by
IAN HAY

Publishers
since 1812

HURST & BLACKETT, LTD.

Made and Printed in Great Britain for
Hurst & Blackett, Ltd., Paternoster House, London, E.C.4, at
The Mayflower Press, Plymouth.   William Brendon & Son, Ltd.
1937

CONTENTS

LIST OF ILLUSTRATIONS

IN THE TEXT

FOREWORD

MY old friend, Stella Vitelleschi, has selected a startling title for her reminiscences, but never was a title better justified. No stranger introduction to a biography could have been imagined than the incident described so movingly in the opening pages of this book. Fortunate for us that the Marchese Vitelleschi stumbled so providentially during his mournful passage down the staircase of the villa at Cannes.

Through that same Marchese, her father, Stella traces her descent from one of the oldest and noblest families in Rome—tradition says that the founder of the line was the Emperor Vitellius himself—a family whose history, especially during the fourteenth and fifteenth centuries, reads like a Boccaccio romance.

On her mother's side Stella is pure Scottish, for her maternal grandfather was the head of the ancient house of Cochrane Baillie, and the present Lord Lamington is her uncle ; so she can, and does, write with equal authority upon the life of the society of three capitals. She is well qualified, too, to speak of an equally fascinating if less formal world, for she is now a London character actress of acknowledged repute.

But somehow I find her childhood reminiscences the most absorbing of all, because they take us back to a Rome which has vanished for ever. With her father a *persona grata* both at the Quirinal and the Vatican her uncle, Salvatore, secretary to the Holy Father himself, our small authoress had the free run of both worlds, temporal and spiritual. You must read how she took tea with Leo XIII, and in particular how, at an alarmingly tender age, she sent a requisition to her godmother, Queen Margherita, for a ration of champagne.

Dr. Johnson once said that a book should help us either to enjoy life or to endure it. Our authoress has had occasion to do both these things. Perhaps that is why she has written her own book so well.

Ian Hay Beith

OUT OF MY COFFIN

CHAPTER I

OUT OF MY COFFIN

MY great aunt, Mrs. Ware Scott, sent a servant to call my father. He had come from Rome on receiving her telegram telling him of his little girl's death, and he now sat in his room with the pale satin blinds drawn down, to shut out the bright sunlight of Cannes and the view of the sea. He was heart-broken and old. He had had his day when I was born, six years after he married his young Scottish wife. It had all happened so recently. But after three months only, I was lying dead here in the room along the passage. It was not so much individual love for me that grieved him, but the fact that I was the child of his old age, for without me he had little left, and he had made so many plans for the future of this new life. I had been born in London on September 29th at 26 Wilton Crescent—my grandmother, Lady Lamington's house.

The memories of my birth were fresh, of the famous Dr. Greig in constant attendance, of my mother's great sufferings, and then of the intense relief, although I, child of the handsome Baillies, the Lairds of Lamington, and of the equally good-looking Vitelleschis, whom the legend says go back to the

Emperor Vitellius himself, was born a meagre, bony little thing with cross eyes. They had to wrap this descendant of the lively Annabella Lamington (née Drummond) and of that ruthless libertine, Cardinal Giovanni Vitelleschi, Field-Marshal to the Vatican armies, in cotton-wool. I was sickly and likely to die. They had to face that misfortune. But Dr. Greig said that if a black bandage were kept on my eyes, preventing my seeing any light for a whole year, then the eyes would straighten without any need for an operation. They listened, and shortly afterwards the nurse came and fixed the bandage securely across my eyelids.

A few hours later, like a carnival doll in cotton-wool and a blind domino, I was delivered to my father in the next room. I was so frail that at six weeks old I was sent to my great aunt, Mrs. Teresa Ware Scott, at her beautiful villa in Cannes, where she always spent the winters. The doctor said it was the only chance of saving my life. It was from here, three months later, that my parents received the telegram : "Dreadful news. Stella dead."

My father had been waiting when the servant came in. He got up and followed him to the room where I lay in my small open coffin on a table covered with white flowers. My great aunt, who was my grandfather's sister, the English nurse, and the undertakers stood round. Behind them the lace curtains hung unlooped, dimming the light. My father approached the table. After he had looked on me for the last time, the coffin was closed. He seemed bewildered as to what to do next, but finally he stooped and put his hands out, and then said : " I will carry it down to the hearse, I must at least do that." My aunt protested, thinking it would be too much for him, but he lifted it up and very slowly carried it from the room. They then followed him as he descended the stairs. He held the small white coffin carefully in his trembling hands. They noticed suddenly that his steps seemed to falter; and as he turned round the narrow landing, the coffin hit against the banister and slipped from his hands. As it dropped at his feet, there came from it a tiny, muffled cry. In an instant my father was on his knees, and all was consternation. My aunt on the landing cried out:

"Stella is not dead. She lives! Oh, my God—she lives!"

The undertakers crossed themselves, and ran down the stairs.

. "Get the lid off—a miracle, a miracle," they cried.

They feverishly began to tear off the lid, muttering and exclaiming of catalepsy and God's mercy. My father tried to help, but was too overcome. My aunt moaned, and wringing her hands, exclaimed:

"Quickly, quickly, don't you see, she'll suffocate."

The same thought was in the minds of all; would they be in time?

There came a cry in a different language. It came from the English nurse.

"Stop!—the bandage!" And with that she hurried upstairs again and along the passage, whilst the others went on prising and muttering and exclaiming.

They were wrenching the last little brass tacks out from the coffin when the English nurse, clothed in white linen and much starched, fell upon them. She thrust her hands with something black in them into the coffin, so that when I was taken out my eyes were already covered from the light by the black bandage, held there by the English nurse's very capable hands.

And so I began life for the second time.

After this they took me to Rome. But this was a very different journey, full of plans for my full recovery and future.

Little by little I grew stronger, and one special morning, several months later, a doctor took off the bandage, and for the first time since my birth I looked round with wondering straight brown eyes at my family now anxiously assembled in the drawing-room for that occasion.

My father laughed and lifted me from my mother's lap. He held me high and stared at me, while the light poured in through the tall balconied windows. From that moment, I think, my father saw in me his own spirit, which, in his mind, was to equal his in a gay world now almost gone. He was mistaken. These worlds are so torn apart, that no will of my father's can bridge them.

When he married, he had left the Palazzo Vitelleschi, and we now inhabited the second story of the Palazzo Massimo. The windows of one side of the palace looked out upon the statue of Marcus Aurelius, which is on the Capitol. I think my father must often have glanced, as I did later, at the statue and pondered with sadness on the quick downfall of glory of another famous life, which a previous, superb monument had perhaps commemorated there. It is said that the effigy of our ancestor, Cardinal Giovanni Vitelleschi, in solid gold and seated on a marble horse, had stood there. An inscription read :

"*A Giovanni Vitelleschi, patriarca D'Alessandria, terzo padre della citta dopo Romolo.*" They say it had been torn down, after his miserable death, to be replaced by a statue of Marcus Aurelius. It is at least certain that the grateful citizens had such a statue built to the Field-Marshal of the Vatican armies, who was secretary and Legate to Pope Eugene IV, and also Patriarch of Alexandria, Governor of Rome, Archbishop of Palestrina, Archbishop of Florence, Defeater of the Orsini, the Colonna, the Savelli, every enemy of the Pope, and creator of our motto "*Mitis sed ferox.*" He was publicly acclaimed "the third Father of the City after Romulus." If those citizens later changed their minds concerning him, that was only in the natural way of things.

He was no ordinary man. He started young, impatient as all the Vitelleschis are, to begin his career and get all he could out of life. He became a lieutenant under the famous condottiere Tartaglia, but he soon forsook this. His keen eye had noted, no doubt, better scope for his ambitions at the Vatican, where he might obtain the scarlet robes of a Cardinal, and to be a Cardinal in those days meant practically unlimited power. He was appointed by Pope Martin V to be Master of Ceremonies, and later his Chamberlain. He studied and wrote nature poetry. For the time being he fashioned his diplomacy, and learnt the ways of the papal court. When Martin V died, and the weakling Eugene IV was compelled to abandon the Vatican and go to Florence, Giovanni was quite ready to take command.

He defeated in a series of brilliant victories each of those families warring against the Vatican. He restored the absolute sovereignty of the Pope, and built up his administration in Rome. Here he now lived, in splendour at the Castel Sant Angelo. He was created Cardinal and Governor of Rome.

The citizens, glad of his jurisdiction and crazy for his honour, continually organised ceremonies and processions in his name. They gave the people of his birthplace, Corneto, the privileges of Roman citizens. They even set him up in gold, and his horse in marble, at the Capitol. He was received everywhere as a king, as befitted the legate of the mighty temporal prince he had restored. The Pope, however, remained in Florence.

Giovanni governed Rome with zest and wit. He believed in fresh air. The odd spectacle of masons building windows and housewives daily opening them in the midst of the huddled, stenching, medieval part of the city, was often seen. Never before had the Romans enjoyed such health.

There was by the Tiber the Città Leonina, a slum of disease and crime, now desolate. This worried Giovanni. He thought, and followed up the idea of Romulus before him. He took the criminals from the prisons and loosed them here, giving them freedom within its limits. They were to pay no taxes nor observe any law. They would have to fend for themselves. He shut the gates on them and left them. It is said that after a time, the Città Leonina became the most terribly law-abiding and moral district in Rome. Giovanni, by the grace of God, took great pleasure in this.

He seems to have been a man of proud and lively spirit, and great personal individuality. He was so out of the ordinary that he was ruthless to the point of jest with his equals, yet kind to the poor. We can

hardly guess at some of his desperate humours. He
spent his time between the Castel Sant Angelo and
the palace he had built at Corneto. He had civic
transactions, ecclesiastical ceremonies, intrigues, no
doubt, to occupy him. But it is of certain of his
nights that we hear. He delighted in the company
of women. On one occasion he sent a note summoning a lady and her husband to dine with him at his
palace. They accepted. When dinner was announced
he indicated the chair on his left for the husband, on
his right for the lady. The banquet progressed
without any incident. Towards the end the cardinal
lifted his glass, half turning, to the lady. A lever
somewhere was moved, and the husband, suddenly
and without a sound, fell through the oubliette and
thence to the dark Tiber beneath. The cardinal,
turning again, set down his glass. He and the lady
were alone now.

It was to these two palaces and such scenes that
Giovanni rode of an evening on his superb white
horse. He was reputed the finest horseman in the
campagna. He had had wide, shallow steps built in
the palace of Corneto, which his horse could ascend
easily ; and, therefore, he could gallop without delay
from courtyard to balcony, from balcony to balcony ;
and it is said his mount had as fiery a spirit as his
own. As he careered through the plain to Corneto,
his scarlet robe flapping across his horse's white
flanks, he must (like Metzengarstein) have appeared
terrible, but full of splendour.

News of this despot began to reach Florence. He
was said to have become " excessive." Cardinal
Scarampi and others whispered in the Pope's ear,
as he sat there in uneasy retreat. It was not of the

B

great ramps, nor the oubliette under the chair that they spoke. Such private matters might be condoned in view of the wrath to come. It was of more urgent scandals that they murmured. He was intriguing with René d'Anjou to dispossess King Alphonse of Aragon and Naples. He had conspired with Piccinino against the Florentines themselves. They leant closer and, in the Pope's ear, they breathed that he aimed to become an independent ruler.

It is impossible to say how far the Pope acquiesced. Cardinal Scarampi had further secret talk with Antonio Rido, Governor of Sant Angelo. They understood each other. Antonio Rido had long feared, and so hated, Giovanni.

Four regiments of his soldiers had already crossed the bridge. They marched out on some expedition towards Umbria. Giovanni turned his horse to go with them. Rido called out to him. He swung round and rode back under the arch. The portcullis dropped. He was dragged from his horse, wounded and bound; while dupes reassured his clamouring bodyguard in the Pope's name. He watched through the portcullis as they dispersed them. They then took him down the steps of his castle to a cell.

He stayed there for two weeks. On 11th April, 1440, when his guard came in, he said: "A man like myself should not be taken prisoner; but if he is, he releases himself." He then put his poisoned ring to his lips, and died suddenly in great agony.

They showed little respect for his dead body. It was taken to the Church of Our Lady of Minerva and exposed there with head, hands, legs and feet naked, in token of disgrace. A few days after, his body was restored to his relatives, who buried it with honour at

Corneto ; and later the Popes acknowledged in writing his great services and cleared his reputation.

The origin of the idea that we Vitelleschis have descended from the Emperor Vitellius, comes from our coat of arms, which consists of the Roman imperial eagle surmounting two calves, below the calves is a pool, and swimming in the pool is a fish.

According to what I have been told, the original coat of arms was the eagle and the calves. Calf in Italian is *vitello*, and the ancient family name as written in the old documents of 1300 was in Latin *Vitellescus* (son of the calf), and later in Italian became *Vitelleschi*. Hence the supposition of our descendance from Vitellius. The fish, as everybody knows, was the hidden sign of the Christians in the early days of persecution, and our family tradition is that the fish was added later on to our coat of arms, as the sign that we were Christians.

I used to go sometimes when a child to Corneto. We put a hamper for lunch in a trap, and with my mother and I on one side and my father opposite, we trotted away along the plain. My mother, very fair and young, wore a long dress of white muslin with a tiny satin belt. Her white hat cast an unvarying shadow on her face. Her fingers clasped the flat, circular knob of her parasol. I sat beside her in my sailor suit and stared about me. My father, still handsome, held his yellow gloves on his knees. In that clear sunlight we must have looked like a picture waiting to be painted by Manet. Soon we saw the *campanile* and square palace of Corneto on its hill-top, while beyond, mile upon mile, were the Umbrian hills.

We would walk up together to the Palazzo Vitel-leschi, long since converted into a State museum. It is a Gothic castle built four-square to Rome, the hills and the sea. A guide showed us into its galleries and many apartments. We were told for the dozenth time how all its windows were different, how the great ramps had been built. We glanced solemnly at the fine pictures, tapestries, furniture, vases and statuary. The cases for smaller exhibits had linen covers, which we seldom lifted. Everything was numbered. A pale sunlight followed us from apartment to apartment, so orderly, well polished, and lifeless.

It was a relief to be out in the hot sun again. I strode into the courtyard and stared from under my cocked sailor hat at the balconied walls. I wondered about my kinsman, Giovanni. I felt closer to him here than in those cool and regular rooms. I touched inquisitively the grey stone.

They have catalogued his palaces, made specimens of his deeds and belongings, turned the men and children of his country into regiments. What part can that fiery man have, I wonder, in our complex problems of to-day? I was quiet as we trotted home in our trap, and watched the sun go down red into the hills.

It was there that my father, youngest of four brothers and seven sisters, spent his early days. He must then have caught Giovanni's spirit. For as a young man and later, he never lost that quick turn of wit, nor the splendid horsemanship, nor the spirit of adventure which his ancestor had had. They were at the Palazzo Vitelleschi in Rome when their parents died within two months of each other. The inheritance was divided, and, as a boy of twelve, my father found himself rich. He used to tell me what mingled emotions he went through when being so young he had to wait in an ante-room while the family lawyer and the others were finishing winding-up their parents' affairs. Through the folding-doors he heard their voices. His eldest brother, Salvatore—Cardinal and later Private Secretary to Pius IX—presided. My father must have been a lonely little figure in that stately room, and curiously out of it. He was slight, but strongly built, and handsome. He had firm, true features; a shadowed mouth, dark eyes. His hair, worn long, was a rich chestnut, and curly. He folded his arms, and as he looked through a pane of the tall window, he mused on many things.

Suddenly the door opened and Salvatore came in. He carried glittering green stones. Francesco looked at him. The Cardinal poured the jewellery into the boy's small hands.

" These are yours," he said. " It is your mother's emerald parure. Take good care of it."

He patted affectionately his young brother's cheek and went back to the conference-room.

Francesco looked at the treasure of the mother he had loved so dearly. They were to him but lifeless stones which meant nothing. There was the necklace, two earrings, the brooch, bracelet and the tiara.

A sudden smile came on his face, which up to the present had been solemn and sad.

Soon after, Francesco went to a jeweller's shop, and pouring the parure on the counter, he asked :

" How much will you give me for that ? "

The shopkeeper, unmoved, counted and weighed them, then made him a low offer. Not knowing their great value, Francesco accepted the offer. The shopkeeper opened his safe and counted out a small bag of ducats on to the counter. He put the jewels into the safe and locked it. Francesco stuffed the coins into his pockets. He left the shop, and half walking, half running through the streets, he returned to the Palazzo.

He tried to sleep in bed that night, but thoughts of the journey to-morrow and at the end—Paris— prevented him. He had determined to go to Paris— suddenly. The rattle of the coach—his foot on the easy sprung step—noise and multiform activity of the journey—the mountain roads—and then the rumbling through the green fields of France—and then Paris—his young footsteps in the cobbled streets—rapid talking in the cafés—walking in the boulevards—the plushed and gilded theatre. Already, in his mind, he saw himself as a young man—in Paris—old enough to manage his own affairs. He turned in his troubled dreams, awoke, and found the dawn creeping in at the window.

Francesco went to the inn where the diligence started for Civita Vecchia. He wore his buckled shoes, knee breeches, a brown long-cut travelling coat, and his white cravat fluffed above an embroidered waistcoat. His eyes took in the bright Rome morning as never before. He swung his hat gaily. He carried no baggage, but the silver ducats were in his pockets.

He sat with the other passengers inside the coach. As they clattered along the road, his slender shoulders were bumped against the corner ; he looked out of the window and saw the hills wearing a fresh purple glow. Fir trees—*les pins parasols*—like toys, sheltered groups of Noah's ark sheep. Broken aqueducts and temples were passed on the bare pasture.

An old bearded shepherd or two, leaning on their staffs like Kings of the Bible, clothed in goat-skin, and their legs criss-crossed with red ribbon, and sandalled. Towns in the hills went by, one by one ; the tall *campanile* towering above red crinkled roofs ; the flags waving at the sky from the towers of their castles. Sometimes a coloured wine cart, hooded from the sun, scraped past them on its way to Rome. Francesco looked out. He felt only the coach's rumbling racket, eating up kilometre after kilometre, until it should reach the marshes. A glint of silver struck his eye. He turned and saw—the welcome sight of—the sea, and ahead, Civita Vecchia—the port of Rome.

Meanwhile, Salvatore had become worried at his young brother's absence. He made enquiries and finally discovered that the boy had been seen at the jewellers. He went there and soon the whole tale was unfolded before him. The jewels were recovered. He had a private audience with Pius IX ; together they formed a plan.

An hour later a detachment of the Vatican *carabinieri*, led by a colonel, galloped out for Civita Vecchia.

They fell on Francesco as he was waiting for the other coach to take him on, and they arrested him ; he protested vehemently, but it was of no avail. The colonel swung him up to his horse and mounted behind him. He took hold of my father's arm unceremoniously, shouted an order, and they cantered away down the street.

On that fifty miles' ride back to Rome, perched on the colonel's saddle and under arrest, Francesco looked a sorry little boy. He stared with disgust at the country-side. The Sabine hills were never so tritely purple nor dull.

He blushed under the stares of the people in the Campagna. He felt uncomfortable, tired, and sick. The ceaseless clatter of the Pope's men on horses behind him, irritated him unendurably. He was almost glad to reach Rome again.

On his arrival, Salvatore took him to His Holiness the Pope, who spoke somewhat severely to him concerning his obedience to his brother, but ended his reprimand with an affectionate smile and his blessing.

My father spent the rest of his boyhood at the Palazzo Vitelleschi. He led his own life, being very much the youngest—an alert and interesting one. He went through his studies, painted, visited, took up music, listened to people, laughed and was full of *joie de vivre*.

He was always accompanied by his tutor, Monsignor Contini, who remained his greatest friend all his life.

My father told me an amusing incident that happened to Monsignor Contini. The latter was one of the confessors of the Chiesa del Gesu, a very rich Jesuit church in Rome, and quite close to the Palazzo Vitelleschi.

In Italy, when there are many people for confession, the women kneel as usual on either side of the confessional, but the confessor opens the door in front of him, and men penitents kneel at his knees, one at a time. On this particular occasion, one of the men penitents at the end of his confession, said to Monsignor Contini : " Oh, Father, I was forgetting to tell you that I have stolen a pair of silver buckles."

" Well, my son," said Contini, " you must promise to give them back immediately, or I cannot give you absolution."

" Oh, Father," replied the penitent, " won't you have them ? "

" Certainly not. I absolutely refuse."

" But, Father, if when I give them back to their owner he refuses to accept them ? "

" Then in that case you will be able to keep them." And he gave absolution to his penitent, who went away happily. When after three hours of hearing confessions, Contini left his confessional to return to the Palazzo Vitelleschi to resume his task of preceptor to my father, he found that his shoes were minus the silver buckles !

My father did not see much of his brother, Salvatore, who was twenty years older than himself, but they all met at dinner, where they heard the anecdotes Salvatore brought with him from the Vatican. One especially my father used to delight in telling me.

A Mrs. Miller of Virginia, Pa., desired audience of the Pope. This was granted to her, but Pius IX knew no English. He, therefore, required his secretary, Salvatore, to act as interpreter. When the Pope entered the marvellous damasked audience-room of the Vatican, Mrs. Miller at once dropped to her knees.

" Holiness," she gasped, " thank you, thank you, Your Holiness, for the miracle."

My uncle translated.

" *Che miracolo ?* " said the Pope.

" Which miracle was that ? " said my uncle.

" Of the sock," she gasped. " All my life, Your Holiness, I've suffered terribly with rheumatism. Having heard that you can perform miracles, when last year a man came round selling one of your socks, I paid him five hundred dollars for it. Since I wore that sock, Your Holiness, I've had no more rheumatism. Thank you, thank you for the miracle."

My uncle translated.

" Tell her," said the Pope, " that she is lucky. I've worn them all my life and I'm crippled with it."

At this time my father was *persona grata* at the Vatican. He would often go there alone, walk about its galleries, the library, or wander in its incomparably beautiful gardens. He used to make copies of the paintings. Once he was seated at the top of a ladder, painting a Raffaello. The ladder slipped ; he was thrown sprawling on the polished floor ; it had crashed into the frame, missing Raffaello's canvas by inches.

But my father did not spend all his time, like Salvatore, at the Vatican. He had a lot to do in town. It was a gay and intriguing Rome in 1850. There was the Opera, the Campagna, the drawing-rooms, the Corso at noon, and above all the many balls, amongst which, those of the Princess Rospigliosi at the Palazzo of the same name, world-renowned for its famous fresco painting of the Aurora by Guido Reni.

My father was a very handsome young man. He held the power within him to do who knows what ? He was already known for his wit and sense of humour. As he ran up the marble stairs of the

Palazzo Vitelleschi at seven o'clock in the morning, returning from one of the marvellous balls given in those days by the old aristocracy of Rome, he would meet his brother, descending, on his way to the Vatican. Francesco would drop to his knee, making a great contrast in his black suit to the Cardinal's scarlet and lace. He kissed the ring and waited for his brother's blessing. Then flushed and eager, he ran on upstairs to his bedroom.

CHAPTER II

WHILST my father went his ways about Rome, he never lost the love of Pius IX. Years later he was to join the political party in opposition to the Vatican, for his sincere patriotic conviction was that Italy could never be, politically, of any European importance until all her separate kingdoms and duchies became united under the single head of the King of Italy. But his political opinions did not prevent his remaining faithful in his heart to the old Roman customs and traditions.

He used always to tell me about the wonderful Roman Easters in the times when the Pope was still Sovereign of Rome. My father used to describe to me so vividly the scenes of those Easter mornings in the Piazza San Pietro up to 1870, that it seems to me I was there myself. He was most realistic in his description of the crowds pouring into the Square of St. Peter's from the narrow streets that led to it, and the arrival of the Cardinals and Ambassadors in their State carriages emblazoned with crests and coats of arms, and with five or six footmen on whose livery was embroidered the arms of His Eminence or His Excellency. The horses were adorned with golden plaques, ribbons, and rosettes. But, as the cardinals and their pomp were an every-day sight in Rome,

28

they did not attract the attention of the people as much as some of the humble *carrozzelle* (one-horse open cabs) within which sat some of the greatest celebrities of the day, who had come from all parts of the world to assist at this wonderful and unique spectacle.

As soon as the Pontifical Mass was over, all those who had attended it would overflow from the basilica into the " piazza," to be present when His Holiness would give his blessing from the loggia, which is over the main central entrance of San Pietro. Nobody was allowed to be present at these big ceremonies of the Vatican unless in uniform, or in Court dress. Therefore, the sight became singularly picturesque when people in all sorts of uniforms of every country mingled with the crowd. This moment of excitement and confusion revealed also one of the important characteristics of the papacy which combines the autocracy of monarchy with the most extensive democracy. All men in that moment stood equal before God's representative. My father would tell me with deep emotion in his voice, of the sudden great stillness that would fall upon the crowd as the loggia windows opened and the Pope appeared in his white robes, carried on his throne by eight men attired in crimson even to their shoes. Behind the throne stood two men holding immense white ostrich feather fans.

Pope Pius IX had a very clear and distinct voice, and as he stood upon his throne and gave the solemn blessing : " *Urbi et orbi* " (to the town and the whole world), the whole crowd sank to its knees and every church bell in Rome rang out. As soon as the blessing was given, the crowds rose to their feet and dispersed in all directions to their Easter luncheons with their families at home.

Strangely enough, the thing that reminds me of this great silence, so reverently spoken of by my father, is the two minutes' silence on Armistice Day in London ; for, although one was for joy and the other is for sorrow, they both have the effect of stirring the depths of one's soul.

In those days, though there were heated party politics, nobody even dreamt it possible that in less than fifty years the whole of Europe would be shattered to pieces.

On the 20th September, 1870, the Italian army entered Rome, and this is the date which is kept as a National holiday throughout Italy, although the solemn entry of Victor Emanuel II was in the following July, when the Eternal City then became the capital of Italy.

The Blacks—the Papist faction—sealed up their *portone*—the huge carriage doors of their palaces—in token of grief and mourning ; all relations between the Vatican and the Whites were severed. But my father some time afterwards received a note from Pius IX. He read :

" As the Marchese Vitelleschi I cannot receive you any more, but as *mio diletto figlio Francesco* you are the dearest in my heart."

My father, from his early youth, had been in the midst of the political struggles. He was a Liberal, prominent amongst the Whites, who finally wrested all political power from the Pope, investing it in the triumphant Victor Emmanuel II. They had been at first a fiery and suppressed faction, the Pope's *carabinieri* had patrolled the streets, on the alert to

disband any meetings or sinister groups of the
Whites. They were foiled in their ardour by a
singular device. In every street, all over Rome,
was chalked on the walls the phrase—*Viva Verdi*.
It was harmless enough to chalk up a pious wish for
Italy's great composer. They could only go round
with a pail and swab them out. For it was soon an
open secret that VERDI would also read *Vittorio
Emmanuele Re D'Italia.*

As soon as they washed one out, another would
appear.

Victor Emmanuel triumphed. My father was
very intimate with the Royal family, and was
amongst those who greeted the King's entrance into
Rome. He soon held offices of State, and he was the
first Senator of Italy. The Senate House is equivalent
in matters of State to the House of Lords in England,
and the Camera dei Deputati resembles the House of
Commons.

His friends had been amongst the leaders :
Mazzini, Verdi, and later, Crispi. The latter and
others used to visit my father at the Palazzo Massimo
and sit or stand smoking and talking, talking,
talking of all they had already achieved and what
they were hoping to achieve.

He did not care for Felice Cavallotti, whose voice
surged perpetually above the rest, and could be
heard everywhere destroying, demanding, and arguing. Their division with the Pope lay in politics
alone ; religion had nothing to do with it, for they
all believed in their faith.

The Pope refused them audience ; but as a King
who refuses enemy suppliants, not as their Holy
Father. They all feared Cavallotti's atheism.

One morning he fought a duel. He was killed, like the fair Earl of Murray, by a sword-thrust in the mouth. When my father heard of it, he said ironically :

" He died where he had sinned."

The phrase was soon in all their mouths. They were struck by the manner of his death. It was a strange coincidence.

But with the years a calmer spirit began to prevail. As the Pope was a sovereign in his own Vatican State, from the day Victor Emmanuel entered Rome, every foreign country had two Embassies, or Legations, in the Eternal City : one for the King, who resided at the Quirinal, which had been before the Pope's residence, and one for the Pope, who now kept within the precincts of the Vatican.

The double Embassies, the one for the Quirinal, the other for the Vatican, sealed the disunion peaceably. It was the day for debates, enquiries, their precious " reconstruction." There was less talk in father's room at the Palazzo Massimo, and more speeches in the Senate. He was most prominent there, and his speeches were known and appreciated throughout Italy.

After an exceedingly full life, varying from politics to travels and social entertainments, which were then at the height of their brilliancy, my father, at the age of fifty-six, had fallen deeply in love with the charming and gifted second daughter of Lord Lamington. She was very fair and blue-eyed, and much younger than he was. Their short engagement had ended in a fashionable wedding in London, which the whole society and political world had attended.

My mother had arrived in Rome, which she already

knew very well, full of new ideas, as England at that time was already advanced in allowing her women more independence, and Suffrage was slowly coming in.

Invitations were received and given; musical ·evenings were added to the political gatherings. She was the spirit, so to speak, of a comparatively new country.

It is odd to think that at this time no unmarried woman, even at the age of fifty, was allowed to walk out without a chaperone, and no married lady of rank might go out on foot unless accompanied, a yard behind her, by her footman. It was thus that my mother at first went out in Rome. Some years later, when I was born, the custom was no longer prevalent.

A pattern of mental, intellectual activities was replacing that of ceremonies and deeds. It was the time leading up to the Proustian epoch in Paris, that fell to dissolution under the Great War. In post-war capitals little trace of a formal pattern was left.

It was frequently to hear my mother play that people visited at the Palazzo Massimo. Music was much loved at that time. My mother herself was no mean performer. She had decided to study for a diploma which usually took six years to obtain, the diploma for piano at the world-renowned Accademia of Santa Cecilia in Rome. So talented was she, that she obtained this degree in one year, which is exceedingly rare.

In England she was the only woman who had the privilege at that time of playing the Crystal Palace organ.

I remember little of my earliest days in the Palazzo Massimo. I know there was a coming and

c

going of a great many people. Franz Liszt was often among them. Verdi still came, but only to talk politics with my father.

Franz Liszt was a great friend of my mother, and from him she learnt much. He thought very highly of her musical talent and gave her valuable aid.

I still have in Rome some of my mother's piano music by various composers, with Liszt's handwritten notes in the margins.

He retained in age the dreamy simplicity and frank charm of his youth.

A boy of eight, he had attended a reception of an Austrian archduchess. She was speaking to him, when suddenly he said : " Look ! I can already stretch an octave," and struck his hand on the keys. The notes rang through the crowded room. But with time he had grown chary of playing music in drawing-rooms. He would beg to be excused.

One evening he came to dinner with my parents, having specially pleaded not to be asked to play. Despite this, he was pestered after dinner with the usual requests.

" Please," someone said. " Just one note."

" Very well," he finally answered. " One note."

He then crossed to the piano, lifted his finger in silence, dropped it to the centre of the keyboard.

". That is your note," he said, and closed the piano, to the astonishment and consternation of the guests.

Sometimes I used to creep downstairs and hide under the piano. There I crouched, breathless with excitement and delight, listening to my mother playing, and watching, fascinated, her dainty feet on the pedals. This always ended by my being discovered and being carried back to my nursery.

One of my greatest treats used to be when my mother told Nana and me to come and fetch her at the hairdressers. The fashionable coiffeur of that day was Signor Pasquali, who had married a Parisienne, whose father was one of the tip-top hairdressers in Paris. It was Signor Pasquali who always attended personally Queen Margherita. Madame Pasquali was a well-known personality, very regal in her manner, and very interesting to talk to. Because of my dark short curls, which somewhat resembled a French poodle's, I was nicknamed "Tootoo," a name which has stuck to me to this day. The Pasquali's establishment used to be in the Via Condotti ; the street so well known to foreigners for shops selling Roman silks, and Roman jewellery. On entering the Pasquali salon, Madame Pasquali herself used to come towards me, and offer me either a small cake of soap or a tiny sample bottle of scent, saying to me : " *Un petit cadeau pour le joli Tootoo bouclé.*" (A tiny present for the pretty curly Tootoo.) We would then go into the cubicle where my mother was having her hair done. In those days women's long hair was beautifully dressed. There were no machine dryers of any kind, so when one's hair was shampooed it always had to be dried by hand ; the process being that, after rubbing the head with a few warm towels, the assistant used to hold out the ends of the hair with one hand, whilst fanning it with a paper fan with the other. If the client was in a great hurry, two assistants were employed. What fascinated me was watching Mama's beautiful fair hair, waving in the air like golden threads, whilst the fans were wafting to and fro.

Although my father was much older than my mother, he was so young in every way, that the disparity of years did not matter. They were finely matched. Both had creative energies. My mother moved as adroitly in the society of her day as did my father in politics.

Hers was the society of flowing dress, the discriminative word, the shutting fan, *bel canto*, the four-in-hand, whilst he was keenly interested in all the politics of the day ; he knew Gladstone, Bismarck, and other epoch-making politicians. He admired tenacity of purpose, and sincerity of belief, even though it might not coincide with his own.

It was a far cry then to the cocktail party and dictators.

They represented at that time two aspects of culture, now vanished. My father was tall, dark, curly haired, handsome. My mother, fair, blue-eyed. She was extremely clever at aquarelles, was interested in history, and played Chopin. My father painted in oils, and discussed philosophy. I still have in my possession an oil painting of his, portraying a barge crossing the Tiber, and on board a gendarme, a monk, shepherds, and peasants in the Roman costumes of the period. This picture gained the prize at one of the exhibitions.

He had also been a noted dancer, and was very fond of music. Many times he had been heard in a music-room or a ball-room, playing Strauss's waltzes by the hour, while his friends danced or listened to him. He and his young wife were both high-spirited. It was enough to say to my mother : " My dear, you can't do that," for her to do it.

Not so their child. I have been cursed through my

life with a faltering in what I aimed at. I have a secret fear of Edmund Lear's " They."

It was my parents' gaiety, wit, and the unpredictableness of their actions that charmed all those who knew them. My mother's tenacity is still proverbial in Rome to-day. Under her fragile appearance, and wistful personality, there existed a will of iron. In the course of an historical book she was writing, my mother needed a reproduction of a picture that hung in a cloistered convent near Turin. Her friends assured her that her book would go to press without the picture, as she would never be able to obtain permission to photograph it. She applied to Leo XIII. He replied that the cloister was infrangible, and that even he had no power to alter this. She then went to King Umberto I, who, after the death of Victor Emmanuel II, had ascended the throne with his beautiful and much-loved wife, Queen Margherita. He told my mother that she had his authority, if the convent would consent to lower the picture into the street. She obtained their consent. A government order was granted to erect a closed scaffolding on the street side of the convent, which was done, to the great excitement and interest of all the people round, as such a thing had never occurred before. My mother arrived with two photographers carrying their apparatus, and these two then climbed up into the structure. The picture was lowered to them by ropes through a window. It was photographed. Immediately after, it was hauled up again, much, I expect, to the relief of the Mother Superior! The photographers then descended, the scaffolding was dismantled, and my mother came back to Rome triumphant.

A month or so later she sent copies of the book to
her friends. In every one was a reproduction of the
picture.

It was the fashion then, as now, to hunt in the
Campagna. Both my parents rode splendidly. They
used to hunt two or three days a week. The meet was
outside the Roman walls. Sometimes it was at
the Caio Cestio monument—a stone pyramid built
through the wall itself, over a man who insisted on
his body being buried half inside Rome and half
outside.

The huntsmen would ride off, leaving behind, to
the right, the English cemetery where the poet Keats
is buried, and where stands Shelley's monument.
On the left, in the distance, were the Sabine hills,
marvellous in all their beauty, purple, as if they were
cloaked with violets. The lesser hills in the Campagna
were dotted with sheep. The horsemen rode by the
fields in which the stocky, half-wild Roman horses
and little grey cows with wavy horns were grazing.
The hounds swept past them, past sculptured tombs,
bases of broken pedestals or a skeleton aqueduct,
across pastures beneath which were the Catacombs.
The Appian Way, flanked by its green cypresses,
curled its ribbon of white to Civita Vecchia. As they
cantered, they might see a gay-coloured cart laden
with barrels of wine making its way towards Rome,
for the hills are fertile in vines from whose sun-kissed
grapes are made those various delicious wines of
the Roman Campagna, which are so noted throughout
the world.

Most of the wine is poured into barrels and placed
in carts to be taken to Rome. These carts are gaily
painted in blue, yellow, pink, or red ; they are as

long as a dray, but go on two wheels ; a stick props
them level if the horse is taken out. Under a huge
painted hood sits the driver. As they rattle on the
dusty road, the burning sun beats down upon them ;
the only shade is over the peasant, who drives lazily
along.

This reminds me of an extremely amusing story
which happened in the eighteenth century. It has
always been customary for many centuries, and still
is, for the Roman *osterie* (country inns) to put EST
(the Latin for IT IS) outside their doors, to convey
to the passing traveller that these wines were obtain-
able there. A French cardinal, who was making his
way by coach to Rome where there was to be a
conclave at the Vatican for the election of the next
Pope—as the recent Pope had just died—sent ahead
of him one of his suite on horseback, to choose for him
an inn where the best wine was to be had. The
cardinal told him to write in chalk on the doors of the
inns EST wherever these wines were really good. On
arriving at one of these *osterie*, the cardinal, to his
great gratification, found EST EST EST chalked on the
door, which, to him, meant that the wines in there
were more than excellent.

The story goes that His Eminence remained so
many days at this famous inn that he missed the
Conclave !

My first memory of my godmother, Queen
Margherita, was when I was four years old and my
father and mother took me to the Quirinal Palace to
see her.

I remember so well being stood on the table of
my nursery and dressed by Nana for this occasion,
in a little white smocked frock and sun-bonnet,

and being told by her to answer the Queen very nicely.

My parents and I drove in our landau to the Royal Palace. We were ushered through many ante-rooms, and shown at length into the Queen's drawing-room by her lady-in-waiting, Marchesa Villamarina, who was also her great friend. I saw a long room with tall windows, where at the end the Queen sat on a beautiful damask and gilded sofa, with ropes of pearls around her neck. We approached and, after a few words, I climbed carefully on to her lap. While they talked, I put my fingers up to the pearls and played with them as if they were a fairy fish-net. Suddenly I said :

" Give me these marbles. I want to play with them."

The Queen laughed and hugged me.

" I will give you some much prettier," she said.

They talked a little more ; then she rose and dismissed us.

A few days later I received a packet from the Quirinal. I opened it and found a string of small pearls and a bag of lovely glass marbles with coloured squiggles in their centres. I still treasure both these gifts.

We used to go to England every summer. It was an extraordinary journey—my father with his valet, my mother with her lady's maid, and I with my nurse, and no less than twelve trunks of luggage. We stopped at various places on the way, to prevent my being over-tired, for I was still very delicate. We stayed the night once at the Grand Hotel in Milan. When I had finished supper, my father came in and said :

" Stella, you are going to meet a very great man. You won't appreciate it now. But later on you will remember it."

He took me by the hand and led me down the wide staircase to Verdi's private suite. He knocked, opened the door, and we went in. I saw a very tall man in dark clothes, with white hair and wonderful white beard and moustache.

" Father Christmas ! " I yelled.

I ran to him. He seized me in his hands, lifted me up and up, till I was opposite his face.

" And what would the little Italian star like from Father Christmas ? " he said.

I stared beyond the white whiskers at the big, grey eyes. I thought a long time, then said :

" Nigger doll."

He swung me down—down past all that height—till I reached the firm carpet.

The next day, in coming back with Nana from my morning walk, the hotel porter handed me a large box tied up with blue ribbon, and on the box was written : " From Father Christmas to a little Star." (As everybody knows, Stella means star.)

I undid the parcel with little hands trembling with excitement, and found Sambo, lying there in white tissue paper.

On our arrival in England we used to go at once to the country house of one of my relations, many of whom were scattered all through the country. My grandfather, Alexander Cochrane-Baillie, had married Annabella Drummond, of the Scottish banking family. She was well known for her beauty and talent, and she had travelled in 1850 with her sister in America. They were so much admired that a two-dollar note was struck in their likeness by the State of Vermont. Her sister was Frederica, Countess of Scarborough, the present Earl being her son. My grandparents became the intimate friends of Benjamin Disraeli, and my grandfather was created Baron Lamington. The old part of Lamington House in Lanarkshire used to be the village inn where the coaches used to stop on their way from Stirling to London. My grandfather devoted the rest of his life to his books and to laying out the grounds and the park.

My grandparents' only son, Wallace, is the present Lord Lamington, and of their three daughters, the eldest, Constance, married Earl De La Warr, relating us to the Sackvilles ; the second, Amy, my mother, married my father, the Marchese Francesco Vitelleschi ; and the third, Violet, married Viscount Melville, relating us to the Dundas family. Wallace married Lord Newland's daughter. Thus, we are connected with many of the well-known families of England, and it was to several of their places that I used to be taken.

I have various recollections of some of these visits. Uncle Harry, Viscount Melville, used to collect tortoiseshell cats. I can see now what, to me, seemed hundreds of them in the grounds and among the rooms at Melville Castle. There was also a grey parrot which was a great favourite with us all. I used to feed him on toast and honey. At each mouthful he would say : " More, please—hungry, please." I must have given him loaves of bread and pots of honey during the time I stayed there. As I put my fingers in his cage, the tortoiseshell cats roamed round, meowing and purring.

At Buckhurst, the seat of the De La Warr's, I remember Margaret Sackville's nursery. We used to play there all day long. It was crowded, like Santa Claus' storehouse, with wonderful toys of all kinds. Amongst them I remember well a mechanical cow that you could milk. The milk was poured in through the neck and extracted from toy teats. We played with it once in our new frocks before a party, and we quarrelled as to who was to be the milkmaid. There was a struggle, a tug-of-war, and the whole udder came off in our hands. We were inundated with milk and water, to the fury of our nurses. The blame was very properly laid on the manufacturers.

I used to go to Lamington more often than anywhere else, and played about alone in grandpapa's cherished grounds. One afternoon I decided to water a flower bed. Grandpapa had fallen asleep in a chair nearby on the lawn. I filled my can and watered patiently the mignonette, tulips, forget-me-nots. I looked round after a time and saw grandpapa's head gleaming in the sun. A brilliant idea struck me. I climbed quietly on to a chair behind him, with the watering-can in my hand. I lifted it up and watered his head. The effect astonished me. He leapt to his feet and shouted furiously for my nurse, whilst mopping the water off with his handkerchief. Nanny came running across the lawn.

" Take this child in," he thundered.

I was swept up, carried off under her arm like a doll, back to the house. I kicked and screamed.

" I want to make his hair grow like the flowers," I cried.

Nobody seemed to appreciate my good intentions. I was taken upstairs to the nursery and put to bed.

Although I spent most of the summer in England, I think I have always been more Italian than Scottish. I was a very affectionate child and a great lover of animals, particularly dogs.

When I was six years old we went to Andermatt in Switzerland for a month. One day, whilst stooping to caress a strange dog which was standing in one of the village streets, I startled him by so doing, and he bit me under my left eye. I went into the shop where Nana was buying some Swiss embroidery. My face was bleeding profusely. On seeing me she exclaimed with horror : " What has happened ? " I told her quite calmly what had occurred. I was rushed to the hotel and my father, panic-stricken, took me off at once to the doctor, who cauterised me with hot irons.

My father and others tried persistently to make me describe the dog, but I refused because I thought they would find him and beat him. Meanwhile, at the least show of temper I was suspected of rabies ! Often afterwards my father and I would pass this particular bobtail St. Bernard, unmolested, and the secret remained between the dog and me ! But the scar on my cheek can still be seen.

We used to spend some days in London before our return to Italy. I stayed, at this particular time, with my great-aunt, Mrs. Ware Scott, at her house in Sloane Street. My parents were with my grandparents in Wilton Crescent.

Every evening my father came in to say " Good night " to me. He bent over my cot and kissed me " Good night." I used to answer : " Good night, Papa." Then he would go out and shut the door. In my childish way I began to worry that every day should be ended with the same term of endearment to one I loved so much. I, therefore, tried to find some new word.

One night he came in as usual. As he was leaving, I put my arms round his neck and whispered :

" Good night, dog."

He drew back and slapped my face. He then went out. I held my breath, then fell sobbing into the pillows. Nana heard me and came running in. She gathered me into her arms. Chokingly, I told her what had happened.

The next night I was standing on the bed when my father entered. He smiled, came over to me, took my small hand, and kissed it.

" *Je te demande pardon*," he said. " *Je n'avais pas compris*."

CHAPTER III

HOW I OBTAIN CHAMPAGNE

AT the age of six I was an attractive and extremely lively child, having inherited the high spirits which my father possessed when a boy. He had passed down to me also his curly, chestnut hair, his complexion, and abrupt ideas and ways. I was fully alive and I was happy.

It was in 1892 that we spent a summer holiday at the seaside not far from the capital, at Porto d'Anzio, a favourite seaside resort of the old Romans ; the Emperors Caligula and Nero were born there and the ruins of Nero's palace are still to be seen, also the moles extending into the sea which were built by him. In more recent days many well-known Roman families had also built villas there, and during the hot summer months used to reside in them. The best known and most beautiful of these residences are the Villa Colonna, and more especially the Villa Borghese whose magnificence is world-wide.

So rich in the ancient times was Anzio, in valuable statues, vases, and other ornaments which adorned Roman patricians' houses, that up to a very few years ago it was quite usual for a gardener, whilst digging in one of these gardens, to turn up some valuable article. The last one, only a few years ago, was the famous statue which has been called " La fanciulla d'Anzio " (The girl of Anzio).

Staying also at Anzio whilst we were there, was
Father Hickey, of the English Dominicans in Rome,
a most brilliant, intelligent, and kindly man, who
was a great friend of our family. Very often I joined
him for a walk along the sands which stretch for
miles, and when the sun shines on them they look
like a carpet of glittering gold. At other times we
accompanied my father on tours of exploration to the
ruins of the various ancient villas, some of which are
standing in the sea. One day, whilst I was playing
on the shore, paddling and building castles, Father
Hickey helped me dig a moat. " Little Stella," he
said, " give me a nice smile as a reward for my aid."
I lifted my face and smiled joyously at him. He
then asked Nana, who was sitting by, sewing, for a
pencil and paper, and on the spur of the moment
he wrote these words :

> " *S*miles that light up eyes and face
> *T*wofold charm of youth and grace
> *E*yes that put the stars to shame
> *L*ips touched with the rose's flame
> *L*oving, winsome little sprite
> *A* Saxon bird in southern light,"
> is STELLA.

Father Hickey read them to me, then gave the
paper to Nana, who handed it later to my mother.
I had naturally forgotten all about it until at my
mother's death, on looking over her things, I found
this little verse, which she had always treasured. I
remember also the small, white-crested waves gently
breaking against the shore. They were some of the
happiest moments of my childhood.

In the winters we always lived in Rome, in the
Palazzo Massimo. This great palace had been reconstructed into three " flats " of substantial size. The

first floor, the former *piano nobile,* where the principal reception-rooms were situated, was occupied by Cardinal Macchi. Our family was installed on the second floor, and the Duca Massimo, who owned the Palace, resided in the top story.

It was not long before I made the interesting discovery that Cardinal Macchi possessed a matchless cook, and I began to consider how I could make closer acquaintance with some of the delicacies which were prepared in his kitchen. Owing to the construction of the palazzo, I found that with the aid of a small basket and a piece of cord I could lower messages direct to the cardinal's kitchen. The message which the basket regularly contained, read : " Please send something for a little girl who is hungry." The cook evidently had a soft corner in his heart for little girls, and the experiment was completely successful ; many samples of some special cake or pastry found their way from the first to the second floor until, alas ! Nana discovered my improvised " lift " and put an abrupt end to its activities.

Whenever I met Cardinal Macchi on the staircase, and knelt to kiss the ring and ask his blessing, I always imagined that I could detect a faint smile of amusement on his face, as seeing me doubtless reminded him of the kitchen episode, about which he had probably heard.

Blessings and religious customs in those days did not, I am afraid, mean as much to me as they should have done. Escorted by my nurse, I used to attend Mass at the Church of the Ara Coeli, which was situated opposite our house, across the big square. I was dressed in the fashion of the day (in a blue sailor hat and a sailor suit). My behaviour was exemplary until I found myself safely within the church. Then a sort of subdued battle royal was waged between Nana and me. I was always a tomboy by nature, and one of my pet whims was to imagine that I was a boy. During the most solemn part of the Mass, when I thought she was not looking, I would remove my cap, put it on the chair by my side, and whisper to my nurse : " I'm a boy."— " No, you're not," she would reply, and seizing my cap, she dumped it on my head again. " Yes, I am," I'd say angrily.—" No, you're not ! " " Yes I am ! " And this went on until my wretched nurse collapsed in horror, and the greater part of the congregation tried to silence us.

Although the outward ceremonies did not mean much to me, I was full of absolute faith and believed that any prayer I made fervently would be answered.

At this particular time one of the painful symptoms of my mother's illness was attacks of violent blood-spitting, which naturally weakened her terribly, and terrified my father. Provided I was watched from our dining-room window, I was allowed to go to the church of the Ara Coeli alone. So one day, I doffed my sailor cap and told Nana that I was going to church to make a very special prayer. I ran up the many steps of the church and, on entering it, I made my way straight to the statue of St. Anthony, which was surrounded with votive offerings of all kinds, including jewels and crutches, which were there to prove that the donors' prayers to the saint had been answered. I don't think that any prayer has ever been made with more faith and fervour than mine that day. " St. Anthony," I said, " if you make

Mama better, so that she never spits any more blood, I will give you a beautiful silver heart tied up with red ribbon, which I shall buy out of the twenty lire a month which I am given for my gloves and shoes. I give you five weeks ; if by then she has had no more hæmorrhages, I shall understand you have listened to me, and I will bring you the heart."

I rose up from my knees and, with perfect confidence that the saint would hear my prayer, I drew a deep breath of happiness as I stood on the top of the steps before descending. I remember so well all the details of that afternoon ; it was a glorious Roman sunset as I came out of the church, and the whole Campidoglio on my left seemed bathed in gold.

Days passed and weeks passed. Both Doctor Marchiafava and Montechiari were surprised and delighted that all traces of bleeding seemed to have vanished so entirely and so suddenly. My father's careworn expression had changed to one of radiance. I used to hear him speaking to the doctors, asking the medical explanation of such a miracle. They answered evasively, and muttered phrases about incomprehensible nervous factors in highly strung natures such as my mother's. The only one who was calm in all this was myself. I was the only one who knew the truth ! And each night, when in my bed, and the light was turned out, I whispered, with my face buried in my pillow : " St. Anthony, thank you."

The five weeks passed. A few days later I told Nana that I had to go to buy a heart for St. Anthony because he had granted a request of mine. Off we

ONE OF LISZT'S LETTERS TO THE AUTHOR'S MOTHER WHILST
SHE WAS HIS PUPIL.

went, and I bought a lovely silver heart for five
lire, and a yard of red ribbon for one lire! I must
remind anyone who reads this book that in those days
my Russian leather boots used to cost only twelve
lire! This is to explain why the twenty lire I was
given a month for my gloves, boots, and ribbons was
more than enough, and enabled me to buy other
things.

Having tied the ribbon on to the heart, I told Nana
I wanted to go alone to give it to St. Anthony. So
she left me at the foot of the steps, which I ran up,
whilst she went home. I crossed the nave of the
church and went to the sacristy, where I asked a
nice round-face monk to come and hang my votive
offering to St. Anthony wherever there was room for
it. He brought a ladder, which he leant against the
pillar nearest to St. Anthony's statue, and taking
my little heart in his hands, he mounted the steps
and placed it amongst many others at the top of the
pillar. He descended, and returned to the sacristy
with his ladder, leaving behind him a rapturously
happy little girl, who, after a few minutes' thanksgiving, returned home.

I was playing with my dolls in the nursery when
about an hour after my return from the church, the
whole household was in a turmoil and consternation.
Mama was having one of the worst attacks of
bleeding she had ever had. I shall never forget the
horror that overcame me; my anger knew no
bounds. Without losing a moment, I snatched my
cap up in my hands, and screaming to Nana: " I
shall kill St. Anthony for this," I dashed out of the
house, back to the church, and literally blew into
the sacristy. I got hold of the same monk, shook

him, and with my words falling over themselves, I told him all the story and that I must have my heart back. We bustled through the church with his ladder, he getting redder and redder as my invectives against St. Anthony became more and more violent. By the time he had unhooked my heart from the pillar and was descending, Nana arrived breathlessly on the scene. The heart was given back to me, and I clutched it desperately in my hand, as I sobbed convulsively all the way back home.

Nana tried in vain to comfort me, and explained to me that perhaps the miracle was that after such a bad attack, Mama was still alive. She soothed me, and told me that our prayers are always answered in the best way for us and for those we love, though sometimes in appearance they seem to be unanswered. And, oddly enough, after one or two more attacks my mother did stop having them, and they never recurred once during the remainder of her lifetime. But on account of her health we left Rome that summer earlier than usual, as she always felt better in her own country. As this somewhat upset the family plans, it was necessary for my father, myself, my nurse, and his valet, and our twelve trunks to go to an hotel on our arrival in London. My father chose the small Deane Hotel in Albemarle Street, which belonged to Mr. Deane, who had been a butler in the family and had married the housekeeper. So naturally, whenever it was impossible to be put up by some member of the family, one used to go there.

Nana used to take me out every morning in Hyde Park, where I used to delight in watching the riders cantering up and down Rotten Row. One particular morning, as we returned for lunch, we found the hotel in a great tumult. Mr. Deane was in my father's room, where he had summoned the staff, and was questioning them concerning a five-pound note which my father had left on his dressing-table with other articles. When he returned to his room after breakfast there was no sign of the five-pound note, though nothing else had gone.

I feel I must explain that, in those days, living in a small hotel where one was well known by the manager, was very much like living in one's own home, and therefore it was considered quite unnecessary to lock doors or cupboards as is done in the present day in big hotels.

My father and all the others in his room had looked in every corner and every crevice ; they were all very upset. On seeing me enter, my father asked me whether I had taken any money from his dressing-table. I answered in the negative, and said that there was no money there when I had been to his room. " But did you touch anything, when you ran in and out of the room, whilst I was down at breakfast this morning ? " asked my father.

" No, Papa," I answered, " only a small bit of dirty tissue paper which I took to the bathroom ! " At once everyone understood what had happened, and the relief of everybody was great, and broad grins greeted my reply. Needless to say, the five pound was never retrieved ! But my father, though he could ill conceal his amusement, gave me a solemn lecture on the subject of never touching anything in anybody's room, not even a harmless bit of paper !

A child of that age rarely saw a five-pound note,

and it did not convey the idea of money. One dealt principally with solid golden sovereigns and silver, so paper meant nothing to me.

My high spirits at last led to my parents sending me to school at the Convent of the Assumption where, they thought, I would be taught discipline. At this time began, so to speak, my first contact with the world, for now I made fresh acquaintances and met with new experiences, and I was eager for any adventure that came my way.

The following story, told by Stendhal, suggests that a spirit of adventure has been one of our family characteristics.

" In Brescia, in 1786," says Stendhal, " there was a Marchese Vitelleschi, a man of surprising energy, whose activities remind one of the Middle Ages. He spent his life committing one folly after the other ; he dissipated his fortune on the one woman he loved, and his time in killing his rivals. A man one day happened to look at his mistress, while he was walking with her on his arm. ' Lower your eyes,' he shouted at him. The other continued looking, and so he pulled out a pistol and shot him. Little things like that meant nothing to a rich patrician, but as Vitelleschi had killed a cousin of Bragadin (a noble Venetian belonging to one of the leading families) he was arrested and flung into prison near the Ponte dei Sospiri in Venice. Vitelleschi was a very handsome and eloquent man, and he tried to seduce the gaoler's wife. The gaoler noticed this, and in his anger shackled him hands and feet. Vitelleschi profited by this occasion to draw him into conversation. Ironed as he was, and without money, he succeeded in making an impression on his gaoler, who from that day regularly spent a couple of hours with his prisoner, who was a man of erudition. They discussed many topics.

" ' What torments me,' said Vitelleschi, ' is that I am like you—I have a great sense of honour. While I am decaying here in these chains, my enemy is a free man walking about Brescia. If only I could kill him and then die ! '

" These beautiful sentiments touched the gaoler, who said to him : ' I will give you your freedom for a hundred hours.'

" Filled with joy, the nobleman left the prison on the Friday night. A gondola took him to Mestre. A carriage, with relays, was ready for him, and he arrived at Brescia at 3 p.m. on Sunday. He posted himself outside the church and waited until his enemy came out from vespers. As he emerged in the midst of a crowd of people, Vitelleschi shot and killed him. In the confusion which followed, Vitelleschi managed to escape and returned to the prison on Tuesday evening.

" The *Signoria* of Venice received news of the new murder. Vitelleschi was ordered to appear before his judges, but he was so weak that he could hardly walk. The charge was read out to him. In a voice so feeble that it could scarcely be heard, he said : ' How many witnesses have signed this new calumny ? ' ' Over two hundred,' was the reply. Vitelleschi, speaking again : ' But your Excellencies know that on the day of the murder, last Sunday, I was in this horrible prison here below. Now at last you can see to what steps my enemies will go.' The old judges were so struck by this irrefutable logic that on the strength of it they gave him his freedom." On leaving the prison one is glad to learn that Vitelleschi handed a gift of money to his gaoler friend.

When I was about eight years old my health gave some concern to the family, and I overheard a conversation between my father and our family doctor, who said that on reaching adolescence I would either grow stronger or become consumptive. Although I did not understand what was meant by " adolescence," I guessed it meant being older, and I was determined to cure myself. If I were to be delicate for the rest of my life, I felt I really had no desire to go on living, so I decided to try the system of the survival of the fittest. I resolved to discard my flannel petticoats and woolly vests, which I had always been made to wear. Owing to the supervision of Nana, this was no easy matter, until, after much thinking, I discovered the following device.

In those days the teaching convents of repute, used to have omnibuses drawn by two horses, which used to go round every morning fetching the various day-pupils. Inside sat a nun to keep order amongst the children, and on the sides of the bus was painted the name of the convent in question. If our bus met another convent's bus, the occupants of each looked with much disdain at the other. We were taken home in the evening by the same conveyance. In the mornings we were warned of its arrival at our homes, by a shrill whistle from the coachman, upon which the nun immediately looked at her watch and allowed us three minutes to descend. If we exceeded this time we were deprived of dessert.

Having resolved what I was going to do, I now

left my room five minutes before the convent bus arrived to fetch me. On our landing was a giant palm, in an enormous wooden tub, behind which I could conceal myself without fear of discovery. In this secret hiding-place I hastily disrobed, deposited the superfluous garments, re-donned the rest of my clothes, and hurried down to take my place in the bus—and away we went! I used to put them on again on my return home in the evening, before ringing our landing door-bell, so that nobody should discover my misdeeds. Looking back, I believe it had its good effects because I certainly became stronger, and never since have I worn flannel or woollen undergarments.

Our uniforms at the convent were navy blue serge dresses, over which we wore black serge pinafores at classes. When we went out in the gardens we used to wear over our shoulders red flannel capes, bordered with black velvet ribbon, which were called " capulets " and could be turned into hoods for our heads when we wanted. As we ran about the beautiful convent gardens in and out amongst the trees, we resembled a lot of Little Red Riding Hoods.

One day whilst we were playing Hide and Seek, the nun who was looking after us, came to tell us recreation time was over. As she approached I called out : " The Wolf, the Wolf, beware, beware ! " Naturally all children of all countries know the story of Little Red Riding Hood, so with peals of laughter and clapping their hands with glee, all my companions ran and hid behind the trees and bushes. Needless to say we were all marched back in disgrace, and I was severely scolded.

Despite the sober atmosphere of the convent, not a very long time passed before I became involved in more, and various kinds of mischief, and in conflict with the Mother Superior who, before taking her vows, had been a very well-known lady-in-waiting of the Queen Marie Cristina of Spain. There was · trouble, for instance, when I exchanged apricots for liquorice—especially as the apricots were not mine to exchange. It was the custom to give children large sticks of hard liquorice, which were considered to exercise a beneficial influence on their health and general well-being. Mine I used to wrap in a handkerchief in my pocket, and produce as, and when, required. However, my mother objected to the sticky mess, and the liquorice was stopped. But I was very fond of it and determined to have it. That I could only achieve through the system of " swopping "; but I had nothing to " swop "— until one of my school friends showed me a way out of the difficulty. In our convent garden stood a magnificent apricot tree, loaded at the time with splendid fruit. " If you'll give me some apricots, I'll give you some liquorice," said my friend. Without hesitation, I scaled the tree, and began to shake the branches, the ripe fruit tumbling to the ground by the score. All might have been well, but for a nun, who witnessed the theft, scolded me, and reported the crime to the Mother Superior, who sent for me.

" Stella, do you know that stealing is against God's commandments ? " she said sternly.

" I don't know that," I replied, " but what I do know is that God planted that tree there, and that he intended the fruit to be eaten. *Je considere que je fais mon devoir envers le bon Dieu,"* I concluded.

I do not remember how I was punished for that offence, but the retribution earned by another of my misdemeanours still rests in my memory. We were served at school with an innocent beverage that was known as *l'Abondance* (wine diluted with water), and another girl and myself conceived the notion that it would be very amusing to flavour it with a liberal addition of salt. To do this we had to plan out how to get to the refectory when it was empty, and the long tables laid for our lunch. We managed this with some difficulty, and when we were all seated for our meal, the fun began. Some spluttered, some choked, some swallowed quickly and felt sick. The nun, seeing this extraordinary behaviour, walked round the tables enquiring what was the matter. Hearing bitter complaints about *l'Abondance* she tasted it, and her expression clearly revealed what her feelings were! Who did it? No one volunteered any information. Very well, then, the whole class would be punished. At this ultimatum, our consciences pricked us; we both stood up, admitting our crime. Our punishment was to consume a big spoonful of salt. Unpleasant, but harmless! We realised then the sufferings of our victims.

During school holidays in the summer, I used to be sent with Nana to Viareggio, the fashionable seaside resort near Pisa; it is world-renowned for its sands, and pine forest. My father used to come and see me during week-ends. It was here that I had whooping-cough, and happily for me, a little friend of mine, Corradino, the son of the Marchese d'Aieta, had it at the same time; so we whooped together, and we were exiled with our nurses to an uninhabited part of the shore. A small placard was put up by the bathing establishment—" *Bambini contagiosi* "—infectious children—so that nobody should approach us.

It was at this same Viareggio, much later, when I was fifteen, that I fell violently in love with the handsome Count of Turin, the present King of Italy's cousin, who was a great friend of my father, and whom we used to meet every day at the Bagni Felice, the smart bathing establishment where everybody of importance met. My father noticed this, did not say a word to me, but took me away at three hours' notice to Paris, where he treated me to every kind of entertainment, and within a week my desperate love was cured, thanks to my father's great wisdom.

When I had completely recovered from whooping-cough, I went as usual to England to visit our relations, which I greatly enjoyed.

When I was about ten years of age I stayed on one occasion with my grandmother, Lady Lamington, in London, at her house, 26 Wilton Crescent. She was a very stately, dignified figure, in a white cap, a beautiful, heavy black moiré dress, with a valuable white lace collar and cuffs. Her hair was pure silver, her face had retained much of the beauty of her youth, and her dark blue eyes had not lost their lustre. One summer afternoon two visitors were announced : Mrs. Gould (a well-known American hostess) and her daughter who was about eight years old. We children soon got tired of the conversation of our elders, and we began to fidget and to long for some diversion.

" Would you like to come and play with me ? "
I asked the other little girl—Marjorie, her name
was. And on receiving her assent, I led her to a
flat roof, which we called the " Leads." Here there
were a few plants in pots, in addition to several
chairs. It was the place where one sometimes had
tea on a very hot day. " Let's water the plants,"
I suggested.

Now Miss Gould was very daintily attired in
pink ; pink shoes and socks, a pink silk frock
adorned with Valenciennes lace, and a silk hat,
also pink, decorated with the same fragile material.
Hardly suitable for a romp. I, on the other hand,
always wore a plain brown holland pinafore
which would stand a substantial amount of rough
treatment.

We alternately filled the can from the tap nearby,
watered the plants, and pressed the wet earth with
our little hands. We also thought it a great idea to
transplant some of the flowers into empty pots
standing there in a corner.

At the end of about three-quarters of an hour,
while we were still heartily enjoying ourselves, a
footman interrupted our play to inform us that we
were to return to the drawing-room. We descended ;
both of us were as black as sweeps ; Marjorie's
dress was torn to shreds, her hat unrecognizable.
" Mama ! " she exclaimed, " I have had a lovely
time." Mrs. Gould, a very smart woman, said
" Oh ! " and collapsed on to the chair, in horror at
the state of her small daughter.

" Stella ! " cried my grandmother, rising from the
sofa. " You disgraceful child—Marjorie's dress is
ruined ! "

" Grandma," I asked, " what is a frock compared with happiness ? "

My grandmother was speechless, but Mrs. Gould suddenly discovered humour in the situation and, laughing heartily, said : " Lady Lamington, your granddaughter is right."

Until I was seventeen I spent my winters in Rome and went daily to the convent. One of the pupils there was Anna Letizia Pecci, called Mimi, who was a niece of Pope Leo XIII. She subsequently married a gentleman of French nationality, Mr. Blount, and now lives a great deal in Paris, though she often comes to Rome, and in the summer goes to her beautiful villa at Lucca.

All the children of our convent were invited one afternoon by the Pope to tea in the Vatican gardens. This was probably due to the fact that his niece was educated there. Changing from our every-day navy blue dresses into our white frocks and white muslin veils, we drove to the Vatican in closed landaus, and found in those grandiose gardens a row of tables weighed down with mountains of cakes, and other edibles beloved by little girls. The Pope evidently not wishing to disturb us in the enjoyment of our tea, postponed his arrival until we had done justice to it.

I clearly remember the impression which the approach of the Holy Father Leo XIII made upon all of us. An impressive figure, clad completely in white, he was followed by two cardinals in their scarlet robes. Behind them was a screen of bright green foliage ; it was in springtime. Suddenly it occurred to my childish mind : the Italian national colours, red, white, and green ; ironically enough the colours of the Kingdom of Italy, whose prisoner the Pope considered himself. The Vatican colours were yellow and white.

We were then presented to his Holiness, and knelt to receive his blessing. When it came to my turn ·I was struck by the extraordinary transparency of his face and fine hands. It was almost as if a light were burning within him. He said to me :

" Stella Vitelleschi, I bless you *and all your family*."

Two things struck me as curious ; that he should address me by my name and that he should bless " all my family," knowing that my father was an opponent of his policy. It did not occur to me then, that a nun had whispered each of our names to him, or that the Pope could bless one of his enemies.

At this time the Convent of the Assumption was at the Villa Spithoever, the gardens of which were built high on wall structures. They were as high as the third and fourth stories of the houses near.

On Corpus Christi, which is one of the greatest feast days of the Roman Catholic Church, we used to march in procession all round these beautiful gardens. We were dressed all in white, with our white veils ; and the little ones of the convent had baskets filled with rose-leaves, which they threw on the ground, whilst walking. The nuns followed with their huge white veils and white mantles over their purple habits. In the rear came the priest wearing his wonderful gold-embroidered vestments, bearing the Blessed Sacrament covered by a big canopy carried by four acolytes. In the gardens at different points were erected three altars, decorated most beautifully with flowers and candles. The Blessed

E

Sacrament was carried to each of these altars in turn, the choir chanting all the time, and the best-known choirs were chosen for these occasions. All the people in the houses surrounding the convent would decorate their windows in scarlet and gold, and watch the procession as it passed. This feast · was generally in June, when gardens in Italy are a mass of beautiful flowers and it was indeed a most wonderful sight, and many visitors of all creeds tried to see one of these processions, if they were in Rome at the time.

A familiar sight in Rome—and it could still be seen up to a few years ago—were the goats from the Roman Campagna, which, led by their goatherds, used to pass through the streets of the capital at about seven o'clock in the morning. A tinkling of bells and the peculiar cries of the goatherds heralded their arrival. People who wanted goats' milk—it was very popular on account of its reputation for being very nutritious—then emerged from their houses. The goats were called to a halt and milked then and there.

My father once told me an amusing story about those goats. He was about thirty years of age at the time. He had decided to paint a picture of the goats being milked in the street, and at seven o'clock one morning he was ready with his paints and brushes, his canvas, and camp-stool. He had settled himself comfortably, and had begun work, when one of the herdsmen came to him and demanded payment for the "artist's models." My father retorted that as the goats were there in any case, in the ordinary course of their business, he would not dream of paying.

" *Niente pagare, niente pintare!* " (No pay, no painting), announced the goatherd. Without further argument, he gave a long-drawn whistle, and the goats scrambled to their feet and galloped off, leaving my father sitting in the middle of the square in the centre of an angry crowd of maids, who were holding in their hands half-filled jugs, and abusing him as the unwitting cause of the poor measure which they had received.

In the early mornings of springtime the streets of Rome heard the musical cry of another type of itinerant salesman. He was the driver of a horse and cart and went from place to place selling *fiaschi* (glass flagons covered in straw basket-work) of *Acqua Acetosa*. Acqua Acetosa is the name of a well, situated on the outskirts of the city. It is said to have been first discovered by one of the Popes. To-day it is surrounded by a number of buildings, and a modern " pump room " has been erected over the spring.

When I was a little girl my mother used to take me to this well in the Roman Campagna for a drive. In those days we could see the local peasants filling their earthenware pitchers and *fiaschi* at the simple, ordinary well-head. The water was found to contain properties which exercise a purifying effect on the blood. Nowadays it is brought to Rome by motor lorry, and sold in the pharmacies in sealed bottles.

Poussin, who is famous for his pictures of Roman landscapes, also painted a beautiful picture of the lovely little valley of Acqua Acetosa.

One of the picturesque spectacles was that of the *balie* (the wet-nurses, of whom there were so many in Rome at that time), who on sunny mornings

could be seen strolling on the Pincio with their
charges. They were instantly recognizable by their
gay costumes or "uniforms." They wore coloured
silk-taffeta skirts and, on their heads, wide ribbon
ruches, held in position by big gold or silver pins,
with long streamers trailing behind. Beautiful silk, .
or cashmere shawls were worn over their shoulders.
Necklaces, and ear-rings of filigree or coral were their
most conspicuous ornaments. There was great
competition among them as to who should be the
smartest. Their brightly coloured costumes rivalled
those of the *ciociare* who were the Roman peasants
of *Ciociaria*, quite close to Rome. These *ciociare*,
who were well known for their great beauty and
physique, used to stand about in the Piazza di Spagna,
waiting for artists who needed them as models. It
was a charming sight to see them dancing the
Tarantella in the square, and behind them the back-
ground of the historical steps of Trinità di Monti
on which sat, and stood many girls with baskets and
stands of beautiful flowers, which they sold to the
public.

I remember on my twelfth birthday being allowed
for the first time to taste champagne, and at the
end of lunch that day my father handed me a glass,
which had within it barely a tablespoonful, and as
I drank it, I thought what a delicious lemonade it
was. The taste lingered in my mind.

Some months after this event when one evening
I was saying "Good night" to my father, who had
been invited to dine at the Quirinal, I asked him :
" Papa, will you be having champagne ? "

" Yes, my dear, I expect so," replied my father,
and entered his carriage.

I went to my room and longed for champagne.
Finally the longing became irresistible. There was
a long-standing arrangement providing for instant
communication between my father and myself in
the case of urgent need—for I was the idol of his
heart. The servants were all aware of this, so I
decided to send a message. I took a kitchen tumbler,
placed a note within it, and wrapped the glass in a
rough piece of brown paper. Then I rang for a
footman, explained to him that the parcel had to
reach the Marchese at all costs, and despatched him
with it.

The servant took a *carrozella*, one of those single
horse-cabs which are still to be seen in Rome, and
drove to the Quirinal. On his arrival there, the
innocent man explained that his errand to his
master was an urgent one, and asked for the parcel
to be delivered to the Marchese Vitelleschi.
Eventually, after a good deal of discussion between
palace officials, the Captain of the King's Guards
accepted the parcel and it was taken into the palace.

The Royal party were still at dinner, when the
major-domo entered the dining-room which was
resplendent with its priceless Venetian chandeliers
and mirrors. Gathered round the beautifully
decorated table sat many well-known guests. The
major-domo advanced cautiously and murmured
something into the ears of the Court Chamberlain,
who in his turn, and looking very grave, murmured
to the lady-in-waiting, who got up, approached the
Queen, curtsied and whispered to Her Majesty.
What had been whispered to Queen Margherita was
that there was a most urgent message from his
daughter to the Marchese Vitelleschi, and the

footman was waiting for a reply. Queen Margherita immediately gave the order for the message to be brought in, and within a few minutes an untidy brown-paper parcel was brought in, on a gold salver, and placed before the Marchese who very amazedly opened the parcel. The contents, not to mention the message, somewhat embarrassed my father. The paper removed, the tumbler was revealed and the message within. Queen Margherita, amused and surprised, desired to be enlightened.

The note, in my simple hand-writing, was handed to Her Majesty, who—to my father's horror—read it out to the guests. The note stated : " Dear Papa, please ask my godmother, Queen Margherita, to send me some champagne in this glass. Stella."

There was much laughter. Her Majesty then gave instructions for a palace servant to take two half-bottles, to be placed in the care of my nurse, " To be administered to Stella at your discretion." Her Majesty herself poured a little into my tumbler.

A Royal carriage a little later drove up to the Palazzo Massimo, and seated inside it, was our footman gingerly balancing a glass of champagne in his hand.

CHAPTER IV

MEMORIES OF QUEEN MARGHERITA

MY Nana, who had been with me since I was two years old, and whose memory I shall always cherish, was a Mrs. Amelia Sindell, whose godmother, Lady Herbert, had provided her with a liberal and varied education.

Mrs. Sindell was a woman of great intelligence and considerable knowledge of the world, and she spoke several languages perfectly : before coming to me she had been the nurse of Princess Salm-Salm in Germany.

As my mother continued to grow more and more delicate in health, Nana became more and more of a mother to me.

The Queen knew the important rôle Mrs. Sindell had played in my life since I was a child, and I well remember one touching little incident which occurred when I was about seven. Her Majesty expressed the wish to see Mrs. Sindell, so, on one occasion, she accompanied my father and me to the palace.

Leaving Nana in one of the drawing-rooms, we were shown into the Queen's audience-room.

" Stella, where is your nurse ? " asked Her Majesty after she had greeted us.

" Mrs. Sindell is in the yellow drawing-room," my father replied.

" Come, we will go and find her," said the Queen,

taking my hand and leading the way through the wonderful reception-rooms of the Quirinal.

We found Nana standing by the window, erect, with her hands clasped in each other. She was obviously somewhat nervous.

The Queen advanced to her, and, placing a hand on each of her shoulders, kissed her on both cheeks.

" Mrs. Sindell," she said, simply, " I can never thank you enough for all you have done for my little Stella."

This touching act of kindness made a deep impression on me, and was never forgotten by Nana.

It was about this time, and before motors became the general fashion, that it was the custom of Roman society to drive in their carriages between the hours of three and five in the afternoon. They drove up and down the Corso, the leading street of the capital, from Piazza Venezia to Piazza del Popolo and the Pincio gardens ; this was called *la passeggiata al Corso*. It had the same fashionable importance as the driving in Hyde Park in London during the season. It was a well-known fact that this daily drive meant so much to the old Roman aristocrat, that some of them whose incomes had dwindled, rather than give up their carriage and pair, restricted themselves in their home expenses.

We did not, of course, make an appearance every afternoon—we drove, perhaps, once or twice in the week, as our engagements permitted, or as we felt inclined—but King Umberto and Queen Margherita seldom missed.

. The carriage most used by their Majesties was a phaeton drawn by four horses, which were ridden

by postillions in white buckskin breeches, scarlet
tunics and black velvet caps. Two footmen, standing
on a small platform at the rear of the carriage, wore
scarlet livery and powdered wigs.

As the Royal carriage passed, those driving in the
opposite direction to their Majesties rose from their
seats, the ladies curtseying and the men bowing.
It was a brilliant scene of fine horses, splendid
carriages, ladies in elegant dresses, and their escorts
in the neat, conventional attire of the period—a
spectacle which to-day nowhere exists.

Horsemen and horse-lovers generally were always
on the look-out for the grand team of flea-bitten
greys which belonged to Prince Alfonso Doria.

Marchese Enrico Calabrini, a celebrated character
in the Rome of those days, used to drive a very
showy team of black Arabs. Calabrini, like all real
horsemen, was very particular, not only about the
turn-out of his horses, but also about his own
appearance. All his clothes came from those London
shops near Piccadilly which are so well known to
men all over the world. This gave rise to a rather
amusing incident in connection with a hunt ball
that was being held in Rome. Calabrini had ordered
a new dress-coat to wear at this function, and to his
dismay the date of the ball was altered and was
earlier than he had anticipated. So he telegraphed
at once to London to ask if the coat could be sent
immediately by post. The answer was in the negative
as they could not possibly finish it before the time
they had promised. However, the Marchese overcame this difficulty by wiring again to Poole's and
instructing them to despatch the garment by special·
messenger. In due course, there stepped from the

train in Rome a tiny London messenger-boy wearing
a " pill-box " hat, whose unusual appearance caused
no little comment, and crowds of people gathered
round him at the station. Marchese Calabrini met
him, drove him about Rome, and showed him the
principal sights. Not content with this, he took him
—still in his messenger-boy uniform—to the hunt
ball, where everyone—the ladies especially—made
much of him. This little London lad was the
sensation of the evening—even a greater success
than the Marchese's new coat—especially when it
was discovered he was quite an artist in his way.
When he was free, in the evenings he used to dance
outside the London theatres to amuse the people
waiting in the queues to get into the pits and
galleries. As soon as this was known, he was asked
to do a special turn at the hunt ball. This proved a
great success, and the little fellow left Rome feeling
that he had really known what heaven was like !
I often wonder what has become of him, and if he
sometimes thinks of his past notoriety in Rome.

I was then twelve years old, and according to
the Roman Catholic Church I was to be confirmed.
My confirmation was one of the proudest days in
my life. Queen Margherita again came forward
to be my godmother. The ceremony was held in
our old family home, the Palazzo Vitelleschi, in the
chapel on the *piano nobile*, the drawing-room floor.
The ceremony was conducted by Monsignor Stonor,
a distant relation of ours, and who used often to
come and see us. This reminds me of an incident
that happened once. This same Monsignor was
dining with my parents one evening. In those days
I used to be allowed to come to the drawing-room for

half an hour or so before they went in to dinner. On this particular occasion I was busy sewing, and required another few minutes to finish what I was doing, when dinner was announced. My father, seeing I did not get up, told me to do so immediately. With a sigh, I said, impatiently : " Mon Dieu ! Mon Dieu ! " At which Monsignor Stonor reproved me and added : " My child, you must not call upon God in that way." To which I replied : " I am calling upon Him to help me, and showing Him I am a Christian." They all hastily went in to dinner, leaving me in command of the situation.

Her Majesty, at my confirmation, gave me a gold watch and chain with the Royal crest on the watch, and engraved inside :

" To Stella Margherita Vitelleschi, from her god-mother, Margherita di Savoia."

And during all these long years that little watch still keeps its time.

The Queen did not consider that her duties were finished at my Confirmation, but continued to show the liveliest and kindliest interest in my welfare.

When I grew a little older, it was considered fitting that I should learn something about the art of cooking. The subject was taught at the convent, where special facilities had been provided. The girls worked separately, in small cubicles with high-walled sides. Having learnt something of the theory of preparing food, I was placed in one of the cubicles, given a frying-pan, and told to provide a practical demonstration of my knowledge. In the next cubicle my friend Marianna was similarly engaged, and we talked to each other over the partition. After we had been at work for some time, she left her cubicle to go and fetch something she had forgotten. Presently, hearing footsteps, I concluded she had returned, and a sudden thought came into my brain. Close beside me was a pail containing rinds, peel, and various odds and ends of food—ready for the rubbish-heap. In a fit of mischief, I climbed on to a chair, and shot the lot on to the head of—the Mother-Superior! The Mother-Superior's apparel consisted of a spotless cream-coloured veil and a deep purple habit. The injury which her veil and dress suffered may be imagined! I jumped down horror-stricken at what I had done, in time to see the door opening and the Reverend Mother appearing. I expressed deep sorrow, explaining that the deluge had been intended for Marianna. "I am horrified that you should dream of playing such a disgraceful trick on one of your best friends," was the Mother-Superior's reply. My answer was this: "Oh, Marianna understands, because,—*On ne taquine que ceux qu'on aime.*" (One only teases those one loves.)

I was kept in, during recreation-time, for a week.

The same friend was partly responsible for another escapade in which I, this time, was the principal victim. The convent had now been moved to a villa which had been built by an Englishman whose motto was—"Never Give Up," and these words are inscribed on many parts of the building. There had been a lift, which the nuns wisely deemed to be a potential danger to their pupils, so it was removed.

Marianna offered to bet me a lira that I would not slide down the banisters, which circled round the empty space where the lift had been. Dare? In those days I'd dare anything. Moreover, there was the prospect of winning a whole lira, which meant a supply of sweets for many days to come.

We climbed the stairs and reached the top floor, which corresponded to five or six stories high. To simplify the manœuvre, I removed my skirt, revealing a pair of white linen nether undergarments, which buttoned at the sides, and ended below the knee in lace extensions. The journey began, and I was rapidly drawing within sight of the second floor, when a door opened on the landing, and who should come out but the Mother-Superior. Worse still ! She was accompanied by a Cardinal who had come to inspect the convent. With him was also his chaplain.

The Mother-Superior exclaimed : " Stella ! " I promptly slid off the banisters, and with a crimson face and tousled hair, stood before the Cardinal—in my knickers.

The Mother-Superior looked grimly austere and shocked ; the Cardinal appeared very amused ; the chaplain made no efforts to disguise his mirth, and with difficulty he refrained from laughing aloud. I looked up and cried out :

" Marianna, my skirt, quickly, my skirt."

Marianna despatched the garment· from above, but, alas ! it eluded my grasp, and fell into the hall below. Not knowing what to do, I quickly knelt before His Eminence, in my knickers, kissed the ring, and then dashed downstairs to retrieve my skirt !

There was a sequel to this. The Mother-Superior read me a lecture on the subject of modest behaviour, and enumerated at great length the duties and obligations of a lady.

On the following day—instead of being with the others, I had to remain all alone in a room reading the Lives of the Saints, and meditating upon my sins. My meals consisted of bread and water. My meditation and starvation diet were assisted by an ample supply of sweets, which I had had the presence of mind to place in my pockets before the incarceration. But the hours seemed very long before I was released.

From my earliest childhood I had always had a craving to act ; and on wet days at the convent, when we couldn't go out in the garden, I used to entertain all my companions by improvising monologues for them, in which I myself took the part of several different characters.

Well do I remember the peals of laughter that rang through the convent recreation-room. Even the nun who watched us, used to be delighted and called me her " Consolation," as she said I was the only one, who by my acting, kept all the children amused and interested on wet days. My reward for this used to be two portions of the famous convent fruit tart, which we used to have on Fridays to replace the meat. So famous is this tart to all those who have ever been at the Convent of the Assumption in Rome, that even now old pupils with their grown-up children, and, in fact, grandchildren, go sometimes to the convent to ask for a helping of this delicacy. The dramatic instinct within me was so strong, that I had a real veneration for one of the most famous tragediennes of the old school, Adelaide Ristori, who when I was quite small, was already an old lady. In the middle of the late century, when Adelaide Ristori was at the height of her fame as an actress, she became the centre of much heated controversy in Paris on account of the rivalry between her and the popular French tragedienne, the great Rachel. Champions of Rachel maintained that their idol had received a " raw deal," while those who took the other side, merely contended that Mme Ristori had stolen her thunder. Although the arguments and partisanship continued for a long while, the two actresses afterwards stated that their private relations had always been excellent.

My father took me to see Adelaide Ristori when I was a little girl, at the well-known Palazzo del Grillo. I remember her as a charming old lady with a handsome, oval face, huge black eyes, and white hair parted in the centre. Her head and shoulders were covered by a beautiful lace mantilla.

In private life she was the wife of the Marchese Capranica del Grillo, and she held *salons* where the most interesting and influential people were to be met.

The rule in Rome was absolutely against any member of the aristocracy marrying an actress ; but so great was the art of Adelaide Ristori, and exemplary the conduct of her stage life, that Roman society accepted her with open arms as one of themselves.

The Marchese del Grillo, the Duca di Sermoneta, Duca Mario Grazioli and my father, formed a quartet of very close friends. Whenever it was possible they always liked to be together, and often spent their holidays in each other's company. The four men were ardent admirers of England, English life, and had many British friends. They went to London every year ; they bought all their clothes in London, no matter how small the article of clothing might have been.

It was about the Marchese Capranica del Grillo, the husband of Adelaide Ristori, that my father told an amusing story. Once when they had been in London during the season, a well-known London hostess had invited them to an evening reception she was giving, but del Grillo had declined, excusing himself as he had to go into the country and would not be returning to London until rather late that evening. "Never mind," said the hostess, "come as soon as you can." Del Grillo protested that he might be "very late." But the hostess insisted he should come, however late. The Marchese promised to do his best. Trains were then not so fast or frequent as they are now.

His train from the country arrived in London at about half-past ten in the evening, and del Grillo, remembering his promise, drove straight from the station to the reception. He was taken to the dining-room, where the guests were clustered near the buffet. His hostess as she came forward to greet him looked him up and down, frowned, and said :

"My dear Marchese, but you are not in evening-dress ! You're the only one who is in a lounge-suit —it is impossible ! "

Marchese del Grillo coloured, explained that he had only just arrived in London from the country and that, consequently, he had not had time to change. His hostess had extracted a promise from him to come when he could, and so he had come as he was—in the lounge-suit in which he had arrived. But, seeing that he was not *persona grata* without his evening-suit, he took his leave.

Presently he returned, in full evening kit and

covered with orders and decorations. He again went
to the buffet.

"We are here!" he said, as he caught sight of
his hostess, advanced towards her and very politely
bent to kiss her hand. Then, to the surprise of
. everybody, he took a cup of *consommé* in one hand,
and an ice in the other, and poured them over
himself. His clothes were in an appalling state.

"It is you, dear clothes, who are invited," he said,
"not I. Therefore, I am feeding you, and not
myself!"

He bowed, turned, and quietly walked out of the
room.

What English readers may find difficult to understand, is that del Grillo had no wish to insult his
hostess. He had been grievously hurt, and that was
his method of bringing it home to her. He had been
told: "Come as you are, and when you can"—and,
having made an effort to be there, had been given
the cold shoulder. Moreover, he had argued with
himself, although he had not been in the conventional
evening clothes, at least he had been decently
dressed in a dark suit. He had not worn vivid
checks, nor was he covered in pheasants' feathers,
nor were his boots caked with mud. He had been
bitterly disappointed in his reception; and he
could not understand it.

It was this same Marchese del Grillo who, some
years later, on hearing, what he considered, the unjust
verdict of a notorious case, ordered the bells of the
churches on his property in Rome to toll. They
tolled ceaselessly for some hours. People gathered
round, wondering whose death they were tolling for,
and they asked and made anxious enquiries in the

neighbourhood. Nobody knew, nobody could answer. At last del Grillo appeared on the balcony of his palazzo and said :

" Justice is dead. The bells are tolling for ' her.' "

In Rome there is not that snobbishness in regard to clothes that exists in London ; formality in this respect is less strict. That does not mean that an Italian hostess is not flattered when her guests make a special effort to be smart, when they accept her invitations ; but at the same time she is not horrified when they arrive in a sort of undress uniform— especially if they have a good excuse for not changing. In Rome it is the man himself who counts ; what he wears, or what he looks like, is of secondary considera- tion. The lounge-jacket receives as warm a welcome as the tail-coat. And this is still the case, because not many years ago I arrived in Rome at about ten o'clock at night, having travelled direct from London without breaking my journey in Paris.

It was my custom in those days to go to the Grand Hotel, with which I had a sort of family association, for it was my father who had been asked to open it, and I could always be certain of a special welcome. It so happened that on this particular night, the Hunt Ball, which is generally held at the Grand Hotel, was in progress when I arrived. This ball is one of the most brilliant affairs in Rome and is attended invariably by Royalty, many representa- tives of the *Corps Diplomatique*, and by the leaders of Roman society. As I had lived out of Rome for many years, I had not been to it recently. In the foyer, whither a number of dancers had found their way in one of the intervals, I came across friends, who immediately rushed forward to greet me.

" Stella ! Stella ! Where have you come from—
when did you arrive in Rome—how are you ? " they
exclaimed in chorus. I told them, when they
allowed me a chance, that I had just arrived from
London. I was still wearing the coat and skirt which
I had worn during the journey, and I had not even
been to my room.

" You must come to the ball—you must come and
dance," they said. I replied it was impossible as
I was not suitably dressed, and felt too tired
to change. They laughed at me, dragged me
protesting into the ballroom, and there I remained
dancing until five in the morning. But I must not
digress !

On our visits to and from England, my father and
I often stayed at Geneva, where he had many
friends. These friends belonged to a circle holding
advanced Liberal views, and were in keen sympathy
with the theories of Jean Jacques Rousseau, who, as
everyone knows, was born at Geneva, and after a
varied and exciting life, died in Paris. Speaking of
him reminds me of a charming little witticism
which was made by my mother—a play on words :
Having met a very social young man, who was
more conceited than he was intelligent, and who
had very red hair, and whose Christian names
happened to be Jean Jacques, she said :

> " Il est *Jean*, il est *Jacques*
> Il est roux, il est *sot*
> Mais il n'est pas
> *Jean Jacques Rousseau*."

This verse amused intensely all her friends who
knew the young man in question !

. Among the men whom my father met at Geneva,

to discuss many subjects which were popular among the intelligentsia of that day, were William Delarive, Camille Favre, and the famous Father Hyacinthe Loyson, who, even if their memories are faded to-day, were, at that time, very well known. Father Loyson, on account of his advanced opinions, had been defrocked, and was living in Geneva. Delarive had a daughter born stone deaf and who—it is claimed—was one of the first persons to be success-fully taught lip-reading. On one occasion I sat next to her at lunch, and had no suspicion of her misfor-tune, although I remember remarking on the monotony of her voice. It was only afterwards that my father told me.

It was during one of our visits to Geneva that an event occurred, which profoundly shocked the whole world, and which we experienced at tragically close quarters.

We were returning to our hotel, the " Beau Rivage,'' and saw a crowd rush to the pier facing the hotel. A group was formed, and a number of people were bending over some object. My father exclaimed : *" Mon Dieu, un accident ! "* and told me to wait where I was, and hurried forward to the crowd. After some time, as he did not return, I went back to the hotel, and at the reception office, where I made enquiries for my father, was told the sad news of the assassination of the Empress Elizabeth of Austria, whom my father knew well. They had much in common as they both loved horses and were excellent in the saddle ; both, also, were very unconventional, and disliked orthodoxy and hypocrisy in any form, but were keen lovers of beauty. My father had an intense admiration for the palace of Achilleion, which the Empress Elizabeth had had built in the Greek style in Corfu.

My father helped to carry her into the hotel, after Luccheni had given her her death blow.

We met in Geneva Baronne de Rothschild, whose receptions, in her beautiful villa by the lake, were attended by many members of the circle to which my father's friends belonged. One day, my father, with numerous others, was invited to a big luncheon party, and, hearing that I was with him, she told him to bring me also.

During lunch, peas were served, and although my taste has since altered, as a child I had a great dislike to them. But I had been brought up to take what I was offered, so I allowed a portion to be placed on my plate. But that did not mean that I proposed eating them. It so happened that about that time, the company became so engrossed in the subject of their conversation that I was forgotten, and while the argument was at its height I quickly seized a spoon and scooped up the peas, thrusting them into my pocket. No one detected the manœuvre. Rather unfortunately for me though, I was wearing a delicate, dove-grey silk dress, upon which the least mark was conspicuous. As we left the dining-room to go into the garden where coffee was served, I noticed that several of the guests began to study me curiously, and I wondered what was the cause of their interest. Enlightenment came to me through the agency of my father, who suddenly cried out to me :

" Stella, what on earth have you done to your dress ? "

On examination, I found that the grease of the peas

had oozed through the pocket, leaving a large stain that must have been visible at a hundred yards' distance.

"*Mes petits pois!*" I exclaimed, to the intense indignation of my father and delirious mirth of Baronne de Rothschild, who despatched me indoors in charge of her maid, who worked hard for some time to remove the evidence of my wickedness.

When I returned to the other guests, who meanwhile had assembled in the drawing-room, I found them deep in the discussion of a problem very much in "evidence" just then, which was the scientific exploitation of the theory of *la generation spontanée*. Everyone there represented some branch of science, or politics, or ethics, therefore my presence was completely forgotten. All this discussion was, naturally, quite incomprehensible to me, and I was exceedingly bored. The only word that was not new to my ear was the word "marriage" which recurred many times in this, to me, tedious conversation. Suddenly, for some reason—and without knowing what I was saying—I blurted out : "Then why trouble to marry at all ? "

This remark visibly embarrassed the company, firmly established me as an *enfant terrible* in the eyes of the Baroness, and brought me a severe rebuke from my father.

Another guest, apparently no more interested in the conversation than I was, began to talk to me as we walked round the garden. Henri Pictet was his name, and he startled me with the question : "Which would you rather do—walk barefooted on the snow, or lose your honour ? "

Without pausing to think of the significance of

the word "honour," I at once answered: "Oh, lose my honour, of course!"

The next day I heard that the unfortunate young man had committed suicide during the night. I often wondered what lay behind his question, and for many days it haunted me.

We occasionally deserted the "Beau Rivage," and took apartments in the Hotel National (which since, became the first abode of the League of Nations). It was while we were staying there, that the rain-water tub got me into trouble. Someone had told me that rain water was excellent for the hair, and I decided to put this theory to the test.

I selected (for the purpose of collecting rain water) my bedroom water-jug—this was in the days when running water in the rooms was the exception rather than the rule—and I suspended it outside the window from the sun-blind. Some time later I heard a terrible crash and the sound of splintered glass. The jug had gone through the hotel conservatory, several stories below my window. Luckily, nobody was there. But the material damage was great, and my father's bill somewhat heavy.

The experiment ended very sadly for me, since my father, extremely angry, ordered me to stay in bed for a whole day—the worst punishment that I could possibly have received, for I was like a piece of quicksilver, and never happy unless I was on the move.

In July, 1900, we went to Massa Carrara by the sea for a holiday, and stayed at an hotel there. One night I was sound asleep, and was awakened suddenly by a tremendous knocking at the door of our hotel. As there were no cocktail bars at that time, the doors of country hotels were closed at midnight. The knocking continued, and a man's voice was heard to say : " *Aprite aprite nel nome di Sua Maestà la Regina Margherita.*" (Open, open in the name of Her Majesty Queen Margherita.) This was followed by excited muffled sounds and voices, which gradually ascended the stairs and landed at my father's door, whose room was next to mine. I then heard my father's voice exclaiming in anguish : " How horrible, I'll come with you at once." I was terrified, wondering what it was all about, when a few minutes later my father entered looking ghastly pale, and said he was leaving for Milan at once, as an envoy from Milan had arrived with the terrible news of the assassination of H.M. King Umberto, by the anarchist Bresci, at Monza. The messenger, a cuirassier, had brought a summons from the Queen for my father to go to her immediately. As my father descended the stairs the church clock struck three. I remained in Massa Carrara with Nana.

My father, with many others of the Court, accompanied the body of his dead sovereign to its last resting-place in Rome, the Pantheon, and then left the Capital to rejoin me. It was during his return journey to Massa Carrara that a horrible train smash occurred. Owing to the overflow of people from all parts of Italy who had gone to Rome for the King's funeral, the railway traffic was somewhat congested. Many extra trains were put on, for the thousands of passengers leaving Rome. Some mistake occurred in the signalling, and as the train in which my father was, rounded a bend, it crashed into the other express which had left Rome ten minutes before it.

My father's life was saved by a miracle. He had left his *wagon-lit* for a few moments to speak to a Senator, who was travelling in the next coach. My father's coach was smashed to matchwood, and not a single occupant escaped with his life.

At the end of November of that same year, the Queen Mother invited us to stay at Stupinigi, one of the Royal palaces near Turin. The room given to me was the one formerly occupied by Carlo Alberto, whose charming motto, " *J'attends mon astre* " (I await my star), provided me with a good deal of food for speculation.

We arrived at seven o'clock in the morning, and were driven to the palace, and we were told that the Queen expected us in the big gallery at midday for lunch. I bathed and dressed, and donned my white frock, as I was in half-mourning for King Umberto ; my being the Queen's godchild made it a necessity. I lounged about the room, then installed myself in an arm-chair in front of the beautiful fireplace, where a lovely fire was burning, and I had put my feet on the mantelpiece. I was lazily thinking about life in general, when I heard a slight knock at the door behind me. Without turning my head, I said : " Come in," thinking it was my maid, and I added : " Lovely to be a queen and have so much luxury." Subdued laughter made me turn round, and I was horrified to see the Queen. My feet fell from the mantelpiece, and in deep confusion I curtsied to the ground, murmuring : " Forgive me, Your Majesty." But an affectionate embrace was her answer.

Queen Margherita was a very liberal hostess, and the magnificent dishes which were served at Stupinigi completely spoiled me for my home food, though we had one of the best chefs in Rome. Although many of the Royal dishes were highly complicated and richly seasoned, at times there were simple, homely foods. Often, for instance, œufs à la coque (in plain English, boiled eggs) were served in lieu of hors d'œuvres.

This I remember well, for at the Royal table special " tools " (resembling pairs of scissors) were provided for the purpose of decapitating the eggs. But I was not used to employing them, and on my first attempt so mismanaged the manœuvre, that the top of the egg flew off and, unfortunately, landed on the neck of Her Majesty, who was seated opposite me. My father frowned and I waited for the floor to open, and swallow me up, but this did not occur. The Queen, as it so happened, was intensely amused by my gaucheness, and the incident was soon forgotten.

That was at lunch. The same day, at dinner, it was my father's turn to attract general notice, but he—a man of quick resource and ready wit— succeeded in extricating himself with grace. He somehow or other managed to drop some spinach on his white shirt-front. Seeing it, I endeavoured to attract his attention, and eventually, by pointing to my own breast, was able to let him know that something was amiss with his shirt.

Father, deeply immersed in conversation (as he always became when interested in a subject), instead of pausing to inspect the damage, took his serviette and began to rub vigorously at his shirt-front, leaving on it a green stain some two or three inches in diameter.

The Queen immediately noticed the injury, and exclaimed : " Vitelleschi, look ! "

On the long refectory table at which we were seated, were bowls of choice red roses. Like a flash, my father took one of the roses, and placed it in his button-hole. He said : " The Italian colours, Your Majesty ! " (Red, white, and green.)

The Queen, who was a great lover of music, had had built in the Palace a fine pipe and pedal organ, and after dinner a noted organist (his name I have forgotten) used to play compositions of Bach, Palestrina, and other well-known composers of organ music. One afternoon, we deserted the music gallery in order to pay a visit to Moncalieri, the famous palace of Princess Clotilde, a sister of the late King Umberto, and widow of Prince Napoleon, familiarly known as " Plon-Plon," one of Napoleon I's nephews, son of Jerome Bonaparte. The Princess, who led a very retired life, dedicating herself to good works and religious study, had assembled in her home a veritable museum of works of art and fine paintings ; and to inspect them was the object of our visit.

In addition to my father and myself were, the Duchess Massimo, a lady-in-waiting to the Queen, and Count Zeno, who was lord-in-waiting to the Queen.

We were passing from one gallery to another when the door, which could only be opened from one side, swung to, behind us, imprisoning us in a part of the palace where our cries for delivery went unheard. Our only salvation was for one of the party to climb out of the window, and drop about eight feet on to the terrace below—and then fetch help.

My father was already elderly, so was Count Zeno, and a drop of eight feet was a little too much for the Duchess, who was no longer young. Being the youngest of them all, I was then chosen to rescue the party. They lowered me by my wrists, as far as possible, and then let go. I landed lightly on the terrace, and in due course the others were liberated. My drop was somewhat detrimental to my white serge dress.

We remained a week at Stupinigi, and then returned to Rome.

An event which greatly stirred the imagination about this time, was the arrival of the Brothers Wright, to demonstrate the potentialities of their flying machine. We journeyed out from Rome to the Capanelle Racecourse, picturesquely situated between the Sabine Hills, on the one side, and the Aqueducts and Appian Way on the other. The name "Capanelle," which means "little huts," is a reminder that, once, shepherds used to graze their sheep there. The racecourse itself was the scene, and continued to be the scene, of many brilliant meetings under the auspices of the *Circolo della Caccia* (the Hunt Club), of which my father was a member, and the *Societa della Corse* (Jockey Club), which he had also helped to found. The Marchese was, in his time, a noted and successful gentleman-rider. After his death the *Premio Vitelleschi* was founded in memory of him, and up to a few years ago this race was still run.

To return to the Wright Brothers : their aeroplane was placed about twenty yards from the grandstand, in which we had our seats, and an expectant hush fell upon the crowd as the Wrights' " bird " flapped its wings in an effort to rise from the ground. Eventually, after what appeared as a terrific effort, it managed to detach itself from the turf, and, at a height of about three feet, fly for a distance of about twenty yards. After this " hop," it apparently became exhausted, and " sat down " heavily. The demonstration then ended.

The Marchese was always interested in new inventions, was a friend of progress, and always endeavoured to remain abreast with modern thought. He had been conversing with Senator Blazerna, a famous scientist.

" Man will never be able to fly ! " said the Senator in a voice of conviction ; and his opinion was shared by most of the people present. How much has been accomplished in the few brief decades which separate that time from the present ! How surprised those men would be if they could suddenly return to earth now !

My father did not know what the word " fear " meant, and he had a great sense of humour.

Whilst lunching one day in Rome, a letter was brought to him, and inside was an extremely dirty piece of paper, on which was drawn a skull and cross-bones, and under it was written : " You will be murdered to-day on your way to the Senate." Papa was going, that afternoon, to make a speech on the necessity of passing new laws for the suppression of strikes. I implored him not to go, and to inform the police. He sternly asked me : " Whom do you take me for ? " I accompanied him downstairs, and I confess I was shaking in every limb. As we reached the street we saw a nasty-looking individual looking round the corner of the palazzo. My father walked towards him, stopped, took off his hat to him and said very politely : " Excuse me, but are you the author of this letter ? " As he spoke, he drew the letter from his pocket. The man was so taken aback that he mumbled : " Yes." Upon which my father said : " But *you* are certainly not a striker, being far too intelligent for that, what have you got to complain about ? " After a few minutes' discussion they parted friends !

" You see how simple things are, if one gives oneself the trouble to explain," my father said to me, and he calmly walked off to the Senate.

He was already very well known as an author ; his most important book was *Morale Induttiva,* which caused a great stir. Nobody knew for a long time who the writer, Pomponio Leto, was. Curiosity was at last satisfied, and congratulations poured in from all parts of Italy when it was discovered that Pomponio Leto was the *nom de plume* of my father. His last work was a most interesting History of the Papacy—the final volume of which was published only a few days before his death.

CHAPTER V

CHILDHOOD'S GOLDEN HOURS

IT is strange how some incidents of one's childhood come back to one's mind so vividly. As I sit here writing in my London flat, with the rain beating against my window and not one gleam in the leaden sky, I am carried back in thought to those days of brilliant sunshine and deep blue sky, when, as a child, I played in the Villa Borghese and the Pincio gardens with my little friends. Every morning we used to go to either one, or the other with our nurses. In those days, the Villa Borghese and the Pincio were not joined together by a bridge as they are now. So, in our daily partings for lunch-time, it was most important not to make a mistake about where we were going to meet next day!

The games that were most in vogue for children at that time, were the bowling of hoops and skipping, and to attain perfection, these games required some skill. So there was much competition amongst us. And when we played on the vast terrace of the Pincio, from which is seen the wonderful view of St. Peter's, Monte Mario and the greater part of old Rome, one could hear our merry laughter and joyful voices, in Piazza del Popolo below. As the time approached for us to return home, our nurses summoned us; in looking back, the amusing part was that each nurse walked back with her particular friend; so the charges of each nurse had to walk together, whether they liked it or not. We used to walk home, hand in hand through the Corso, our nurses following.

Well do I recall one particular day, on which Pio Grazioli, the son of Duca Mario Grazioli, was with us, dressed as usual in his Little Lord Fauntleroy suit of black velvet with lace collar. In those days he had long brown curls. He walked between Elsa Grant and myself, holding our hands. Elsa Grant was the daughter of the Guglielmo Grant so well known for his wit, and gift of writing poems in Roman dialect; her mother was a beautiful American whose kindness was difficult to surpass.

Outside the Palazzo Doria there were two *carabinieri* in their full swagger uniforms. Without any word of warning, Pio dragged us up to them, and pushing us up against them, detached himself and said: " Take these girls, I am tired of them." We were terrified; as we looked up at the *carabinieri*, they seemed to us bigger and fiercer than any giant we had ever read of in our fairy tales. But they laughed heartily, and our nurses coming up at that moment rescued and reassured us, and censured our little companion. Italian boys, when about ten years old, generally had for their tutors priests who taught them and took them out for walks, unless, of course, they were sent to educational colleges owned by Jesuits, Dominicans, and other Orders.

It is Pio and his wife, Rufina, who are amongst my greatest and staunchest friends to-day.

Another memory of this period that comes to me, is the Easter Egg parties that the Duca Giulio Grazioli and his wife, Maria—whose nickname was

MILKING GOATS IN A STREET OF ROME

From an engraving

" Nini "—used to give, for us children, in the lovely villa outside Porta Salaria. They were the brother and sister-in-law of Pio's father, and had four children—two boys and two girls. These egg parties were among the gayest, and we used to count the days each year for Easter to come.

Lovely bright-coloured eggs were hidden everywhere in the most remote corners of the garden ; under bushes, and even up in the trees. The competition of finding our prizes caused great excitement, as the finder of the greatest number of these eggs would be given a lovely present from the Duchess herself. This was followed by a delightful tea.

Little, then, did any of us guess what sorrows might be in store for us, and that our dearly loved and delightful playmate, Riccardo Grazioli, would be killed only a few years after at Adua, in performing a great deed of valour. To us who remain, it seems sadly true that : " Those whom the Gods love die young."

Another sad memory of my youth is that of the illness of my Nana, whose health began to fail. Creeping paralysis set in, and unfortunately she was obliged to return to England. It was a terrible blow for all of us ; I miss her to this day. So a competent maid now took her place, when I travelled with my father.

On one of my visits to Paris with Papa we arrived at a time when Sarah Bernhardt was acting in *Lucretia Borgia*. I made up my mind that, somehow or other, I simply must see her perform. The difficulty was to find an opportunity to escape from the watchful eye of my father. I knew it was useless asking him, because he was adamant in his

G

decision that I was not to go to any theatre until I was eighteen.

As usual, we were staying at the Hôtel Vouillemont in the rue Boissy d'Anglas, a favourite gathering place of leading members of international society. My father possessed many friends in this interesting circle, among them the old Countess Rcewuska, who was an aunt of the Caetani, and had been a great beauty in her day. At the time of which I am writing she was ninety, but her brilliant intelligence seemed to become sharper and clearer as the years went by, instead of dimming. She held a *salon* in Paris, that was the envy of many of the younger hostesses. Old and young alike, from all parts of the world, used to flock to her daily " at homes " from six o'clock in the evening, until eight. She adored my father ; I can hear her now, exclaiming as we entered her drawing-room : " *Checco, nous apporte de Rome à Paris, la coupole de St. Pierre sur sa tête et le ruban tricolore autour du cou !* (Checco brings to us in Paris from Rome the dome of St. Peter on his head and the tricolour ribbon round his neck.) By this she meant that my father carried with him the spirit of Rome, so Roman was he, and yet mentally he was modern Italy.

I have so far forgotten to mention that " Checco," a diminutive of Francesco, was the name by which he was known to all.

One evening when dinner was over, my father went out as usual and I retired to my room. After my maid had settled me for the night, I got up and re-dressed. I descended the stairs, looking cautiously round hoping I should meet nobody I knew. Luck was with me. I slipped out of the hotel door unseen.

I walked as far as the Place de la Madeleine, and there hopped on to a bus which passed the theatre where I had determined to go. My heart beat fast with excitement and anticipation at the thought of seeing Sarah Bernhardt, about whom I had heard so much. In those days my monthly allowance was twenty lire, out of which I had to provide myself with boots and gloves, so I could not indulge in stalls or dress circle for my escapade. The utmost I could afford was the gallery ; hastily grasping my ticket, I tore up the stairs, which seemed to me endless, like Jacob's ladder. It is very appropriately called in Paris " *le Paradis* " because it needs so much effort to get there !

It is difficult to describe my feelings on beholding a theatre for the first time—I was dazzled and frightened as I looked around me.

Suddenly the three knocks sounded and the curtain went up. Within a few moments I was completely transported into the domain of Lucretia Borgia, nothing else existed for me ! Never shall I forget Sarah Bernhardt's voice, acting and personality.

In the interval, when I had an opportunity to study the audience, to my horror I saw below me in the stalls the bald head of Papa ! Unkind fate had led him on the same night, to the same theatre.

However, I decided to take the risk and see the play through to the end. When it was over, I scrambled to my feet, ran out of the theatre, took the first bus and returned to the hotel. As quickly as I could, I rushed to my room, and without stopping to undress, slipped into bed and feigned sleep, as my father, on his return, always looked in to see if I was all right. Only a few seconds later I heard my door gently open. For a brief space there was silence, after which I heard the door softly close. I sighed with relief, crept out of bed in the dark, and hastily disrobed. My slumber was broken by visions of dazzling light, and Sarah Bernhardt.

Either during that visit to Paris, or during a previous stay, while lunching one day at the Restaurant Lucas, in the Place de la Madeleine, an establishment managed, in person, by that striking and famous man, Monsieur Lucas, it was I who caused some consternation by leaving a penny tip for the waiter. M. Lucas' restaurant, by the way, was the place at which we regularly lunched, for there we would meet the leading men in French— and international—political circles ; and my father, after the meal, would move to another table to take coffee with friends, or, vice versa, friends would move over to our table. On the occasion to which I refer, Papa had left the table to speak to Prince Odescalchi, and he had also left me to pay the bill. I paid, and out of the change which the waiter brought back I placed on the table *deux sous* as a tip. The waiter eyed it—and passed on. Papa on his return saw the penny and demanded an explanation.

" That's the *pourboire*," I said.

The omission was promptly remedied. I am not quite certain which was the more comic, the waiter's expression or that of my father.

On another occasion, at the same restaurant, my father, after lunch, was deeply immersed in conversation with a well-known French statesman who had come over to our table. Again it had been left to me to obtain the bill.

" *La soustraction, si'l vous plaît !* " I demanded of the waiter.

This unusual form reached my father's ear, and he turned round quickly.

" *L'addition, petite sotte !* " he corrected.

" All right, Papa," I said. " Call it an ' addition ' if you like, but I consider that for us it is a ' subtraction ' ! "

We never stayed longer than a week or ten days in Paris on our return journey, as the many duties my father had in Rome necessitated his presence there in the early autumn.

When in my teens, I used to sit with him in his room in the late evenings, and hear him read to me his speeches for to-morrow. He dealt with all the internal and International subjects of the day. Often I put in a word here or there. It was long past my bedtime ; and I was interested in what he read. He would introduce my remarks into his speeches. Next day in the Senate he would add with pride : " As my daughter says . . ." " As my little girl well reasons . . ."

I remember that once, on the occasion of a students' strike, I said : " You'll have your kindergartens striking next ! " Arguing for prompt suppression, he mentioned my remark in his speech. It was greeted with applause ; he won his point, even receiving letters about it. I became well known in the Senate. One Senator said : " Vitelleschi's daughter beats us all ! "

My father enjoyed as much as I did these evenings in his room, as it was a pleasure to him to watch my reactions, and hear my point of view on his ideas and opinions.

I had been so soaked in a political atmosphere since my early youth, that I was really able to have and express a personal opinion. It interested my father to see the effect of his theories, which were the result of mature thought and years of experience, on a young mind which represented a future generation.

Very often, on Sunday, we used to go and spend the day at Frascati, to see my cousin, Padre Giovanni Vitelleschi, who was the Father Superior of the Jesuit educational college at Villa Mondragone. He was the son of my father's brother, Angelo. We used to lunch there, and after he would call into the parlour some of my young friends, who were pupils at the college, amongst whom was Pio Grazioli, of whom I have already spoken. This school corresponds with Eton and Beaumont in England.

Padre Giovanni, who was my first cousin, was then a man of forty, clean shaven, with very clear-cut features, big grey eyes, and hair turning grey. The reason of my having first cousins of forty and over, was that my father's brothers had both married when quite young, so when I was born, my cousins were already grown up. Looking back, it seems to me that it must have been a touching sight to see an old man like my father, with such a young child, on whom he had to bestow even greater tenderness, as my mother was constantly ill. On two or three occasions, when my mother was convalescing, she was sent to the Grand Hotel at Frascati, as the air is so good there. She was very fond of Padre Giovanni who often came to see her; his mother had been a close relation of the Lutzöws, who are one of the greatest families in Austria, and Giovanni and his sisters Giulia and Maria had inherited the double charm of these two nationalities.

Padre Giovanni was not only a marvellous organiser and an exceedingly spiritually minded man, but he was also exceedingly human and understanding with his pupils and all those who came under his sphere. His death was a great grief and loss to his Order and all those in the college, who remember him still with deep admiration and affection.

He was not the only Vitelleschi who was a Jesuit, for, centuries before, in 1639, the Director-General of the Order had been Father Muzio Vitelleschi.

Frascati has always been renowned, since ancient days, for its wonderful and unique villas, which are difficult to describe, even if one has been there. It is only twenty miles from Rome, and Cicero and Lucullus were amongst those who dwelt there. In the Middle Ages most of the princely Roman families built their summer residences at Frascati.

The principle ones and those that are the most beautiful are : Villa Torlonia, Villa Aldobrandini, Villa Grazioli, and the aforementioned Villa Mondragone, called so on account of its fountain with four dragons (Mondragone means " my dragon ") which used to belong to Prince Borghese. One of the features of the house belonging to this villa is that, originally, it had three hundred and sixty-five windows to honour the reform of the Calendar by Gregory.

Talking of ecclesiastics reminds me of an amusing episode which happened to me when I was about fourteen. My grandfather and grandmother Vitelleschi are buried in the well-known church of San Marco in Rome, near Piazza Venezia and often on Sundays, Papa and I went to Mass there. My grandparents were among the last to be buried in the church as, after that time, it was forbidden by law.

My grandmother, before her marriage, was the daughter of Marchese Ricci, and I still have relations of that name.

My father always wore a black silk skull-cap in church owing to his baldness, to avoid catching cold, as the churches were not heated.

On this particular Sunday, as we reached San Marco, he found he had forgotten his cap and asked me to run back to Palazzo Massimo, just a few yards away, and fetch it. I did so and on entering the church, which was very dark, I saw my father sitting at the side near the front altar. As I advanced I beheld, to my terror, two horns sticking out of his head. Dim stories of the devil taking possession of human beings surged into my brain. I felt sick with fear, but clutching the cap in my hand I again took a few steps forward. The horns seemed to increase in size. I clenched my teeth and reached my father ; I then saw what it was that had alarmed me. Whilst waiting for his cap, Papa had blown into his gloves and placed them on his head, and in the uncertain light of the church the fingers of the gloves looked like horns !

My father had a deep veneration for his parents and I possess a letter written by him to them, when he was eight years old. It was to congratulate them on having arrived in safety at our country estate,

Repasto, in Umbria, without having been waylaid by brigands!

Repasto had been in our family since 1120. One reaches it now from Rome by train within two hours; at the time of my grandparents it took three days by coach, and they used to send a messenger on horseback to assure their children of their safe arrival.

Repasto is a large property in the fertile Agro Reatino, which is the well-cultivated valley near Rieti and Terni. The house itself resembles an old white homestead. Attached to it, is the family chapel of Sant 'Andrea, where Mass is still said every Sunday. In the days of my father the priest used to ride down the mountainside on the back of a mule, as he had to come from the hill town which was our parish. It was in this chapel in the Middle Ages, that the Pope's pardon was brought to our ancestor, Andrea, who had killed his brother.

The River Velino flows through the lower part of the property, and its banks are lined with poplar trees and willows. The surrounding land is extensively cultivated for beetroot and for cattle grazing. The outlying farm-houses are inhabited by the peasants who work on the land, and in my grandfather's time the brick oven was still in use.

The higher part of the property consists of hills and mountains covered with cyclamens of all shades of colour which, seen from a distance, resemble a glorious sunset.

I used to run about these hills as a child, my playmates being the young goats who were busily eating the shrubs. Every week the bailiff used to send us up to Rome a big hamper of cyclamens, which Mama used to adorn her rooms with, as she loved all flowers and particularly cyclamens.

Our neighbour at Repasto was Prince Potenziani, a most intimate friend of our family. My father was the executor of the will of the Princess Potenziani, mother of the present Prince, who was Governor of Rome a few years ago, and is a great friend of mine.

CHAPTER VI

THE LAST POST

"THE greatest present one woman can give another is the confiding of a secret." These words were spoken to me by my grandmother, the then Dowager Lady Lamington, after I had lunched with her at her house on my eighteenth birthday; a very important occasion in my life, for I was then about to make my official entrée into society. Grandmama held my hand as I sat beside her on the sofa, and explained this phrase by telling me of how, when she was eighteen, a certain friend of hers, a few years older than herself, had confided to her a secret which, had she betrayed, would have done incalculable harm. My grandmother added that during her long life she had observed that, most of the troubles in this world, are caused by people repeating things which have been told them in strict confidence. " You see," she said, " it is a great honour to be trusted, and the greatest gift one can receive."

I was impressed, but somewhat disappointed that I had not received a tangible present, as I was somewhat of a child for my age. But since then I, too, have realised the profound truth and value of her words.

She then explained to me the significance of my eighteenth birthday, and told me that all my actions, my words, and stated opinions would from that day be noted and commented upon. By them I would be judged. It was a reminder to me to be careful and thoughtful, and to prepare me for a round of gaiety, which I should taste for the first time on my return to Rome.

As soon as we were installed again in Palazzo Massimo for the winter, preparations began for my coming out, after Christmas. I now began to dine with my parents when they had guests, and so I met many more people, amongst them Sgambati, the pianist and composer ; Conte Enrico di San Martino, Director of the Accademia di Santa Cecilia, of whom I have already spoken ; Madame Chaminade, whose songs Mama used to sing so delightfully and sometimes accompany herself on the guitar. These evenings were delightful and much appreciated by everybody.

William Heinemann, the publisher, often came to dinner and used to entertain us with many anecdotes.

My great excitement was my coming-out frock which my mother had ordered from Paris ; my maid and I anxiously awaited its arrival ; in fact I think my maid's excitement was greater than my own. Never before had we so eagerly awaited the arrival of the postman.

At last the parcel appeared ! It was opened in the drawing-room, where all the household had congregated, and when my maid lifted it out, there was a murmur of admiration. It was made of white *mousseline-de-soie* with little ruches of white satin ribbon round the bottom, a wide satin belt, and the *décolletée* encircled by small rosebuds. It was the custom then for a débutante to be entirely in white.

The auspicious night arrived. My first ball was at the American Embassy which, in those days, was at the Palazzo Brancaccio, the magnificent palace of Prince Brancaccio. From the drawing-room one could walk straight out into the wonderful gardens, containing rare species of flowers and plants from all over the world.

This ball was the coming-out dance of one of the two daughters of Mr. and Mrs. Meyer, the American Ambassador and his wife.

Streams of carriages drove up under the *portone*, past the uniformed porter, who stood at the entrance in his immovable splendour.

In those days, and up to the time of the Great War, all the Roman palaces had their *portiere* (porter) who, every afternoon and also in the evenings, when there was a reception at the palace, used to stand in the middle of the *portone* (the huge carriage entrance which leads from the street into the courtyard of the palace) in his full dress, which consisted of a long coachman's coat—the colour of the livery of the family he served—and a black Napoleon hat with the coat of arms on it ; and he held in his hand *la mazza*, which is a long thick staff resting on the ground, encircled with coloured silk cord and tassel, and with a big silver knob bearing the family crest.

As I entered the ballroom with my parents, I felt rather nervous and shy. After we had been received by our hosts, my parents drifted away to talk to their various friends. I greeted Mrs. Meyer's daughters ; then, feeling somewhat bewildered by the crowd of people, I leant against the wall, watching the dancers.

Suddenly I was startled by a gust of wind at my feet, and before I had time to realise what it was, my dress was swept over my head. One of my great friends, Duke Mondo Mondragone, rushed to my assistance.

" If you must stand round the room, don't choose the ventilator to stand over," said Mondragone, and he took me off to dance.

My mother made a very great effort to come with me that evening as her health was failing fast. It was the last time she ever attended an evening reception.

The climax of the evening at a Roman ball of that time was the Cotillon. It consisted of a number of figures—the Lancers, Quadrilles, Sir Roger de Coverly, etc.—and was under the control of a *Maître de Cotillon*, upon whom the success of the dance most often depended. For the Cotillon itself the partnership was often arranged days and weeks before the ball, while for the figures one danced with anyone. Hostesses used to supply little presents for partners to exchange during the dance, and for the last, the principal figure, valuable presents— such as gold cigarette-cases and brooches—were often provided. The minor presents could be given to anybody, as one's fancy decided, but the valuable present had to be given to the official Cotillon partner. My father had been favourite Master of Cotillon to Queen Margherita, and had continued to exercise this office for many years.

The balls frequently lasted until six or seven o'clock in the morning ; and it was an unwritten law—as at the Hunt balls in England—that one turned out to hunt on the " morning after." But if the dance was held on a Saturday night, it was a " meet " of a different nature. Ladies used to bring with them to the ball a black veil. On leaving the dance they donned it, and went straight to early Sunday Mass, often at the Church of San Marcello, which is situated on the Corso, after which, home to bed for a well-deserved rest.

A considerable amount of entertaining was also done by foreign Ambassadors and Ministers of the Holy See, and among the most popular and best-attended of these receptions and balls were those given by the Austrian Ambassador and his wife (the Reverteras) at the historic Palazzo di Venezia, from whose balcony Mussolini to-day makes his big public speeches. The Palazzo was an ancient Hapsburgian possession.

The receptions which generally preceded the dancing, were invariably attended by members of the Cardinalate wearing their impressive scarlet robes. At the Palazzo Venezia, footmen in medieval livery lined the staircase, holding torches, and remained there until the last Cardinal had arrived. The other guests greeted their Eminences by kneeling and kissing the ring which Cardinals wore over their gloves. These rings were unique, containing as a rule a large single gem—it might be an emerald, sapphire, ruby, or other precious stone—whose value often ran to many hundreds of pounds.

While ecclesiastic princes were present, the ladies, who had arrived in *décolletée* for the ball, draped their shoulders in a small " mantilla," which remained until after their Eminences had left, the rule being that they left about midnight.

At the reception there was a musical programme

and entertainment of a strictly non-frivolous nature. But with the departure of the Cardinals the scene underwent a sudden change: the mantillas disappeared, and the more light-hearted business of dancing took its place.

The Austrian Ambassador at the Quirinal Court was Count Henry Lützow, an exceedingly popular and hospitable member of the Diplomatic Corps. The Embassy was at the Palazzo Chigi, in Piazza Colonna, the beautiful house built by Prince Chigi. It is noted for the famous statues in the courtyard. To-day it is the home of the Ministry of Foreign Affairs.

The balls given by Count and Countess Lützow were among the most brilliant functions of their kind in Rome. Not a small measure of their success was due to the white-uniformed Hungarian *cigany* bands, which made a special journey from Austria for the occasion. At about three in the morning wonderful suppers were served. The guests sat at small tables, having made up their particular little parties, and champagne corks popped merrily. After supper followed the *pièce de résistance*, the Cotillon; and the presents which were distributed at the time must have been worth a small fortune.

Our hostess, Countess Nora Lützow, with her beautiful white hair and young face, and lovely figure, was amongst the most attractive personalities at the ball.

The ultra-modern dance of the day was the Boston Waltz, but the Lützow balls were invariably opened by the Ambassador and his wife with the real *Wiener Waltzer*. The Embassy secretaries, attachés, and their wives, as well as the Austrian guests, danced these waltzes to perfection, and much as we non-Austrians tried to emulate them, they were always in a class by themselves. Modern dancers can have no conception of the difficulties of the " old-fashioned " waltz, and of the long practice which is necessary in order to master it.

The Roman balls were essentially informal ; they were very sociable affairs. There was no official advance-booking of partners—save for the main figure of the Cotillon—so programmes did not exist. Equally, the modern practice of keeping to a small group, or to one partner, was unknown : as far as possible, everyone danced with everybody else.

The Cotillon presents which were exchanged at the Court balls bore the initials of the King and Queen, and were greatly prized and valued. The gifts, as a rule, were in silver or gold and the initials were worked either in diamonds, rubies, or emeralds, that is, in white, red, and green—the three colours which form the Italian flag. For the gentlemen there were practical gifts such as ash-trays or pencils ; these also were initialled.

To-day, in the bank in Rome, I have, in addition to presents from the time of King Umberto and Queen Margherita, gifts which bear the initials of their present Majesties, King Victor Emanuel III and Queen Elena. They are guarded with the rest of the family silver plate.

The ball season, which opened on 26th December, that is, on the English Boxing Day, ended on the last night of Carnival, Shrove Tuesday. Although, strictly speaking, when the clock struck midnight it was Ash Wednesday, it was quite impossible to attempt to stop a Roman ball at such an early

H

hour. Accordingly, dancing continued till dawn, when footmen entered the ballroom and drew aside the curtains. With that, dancing automatically ceased. Taking our veils and cloaks, we went directly from the ball to early Mass, and then returned home in our evening dress with a cross in ashes on our foreheads.

In the Roman Church it is the custom for each person attending Mass on Ash Wednesday, to proceed to the altar on conclusion of the Mass. The officiating priest takes from a golden chalice a pinch of blessed ashes, and with them makes a sign of the cross on the worshipper's forehead.

" Remember that thou art dust and that to dust thou shalt return," says the priest.

One of the most picturesque Church customs in Rome at this time of the year is the blessing of the " new fire," on Easter Saturday, which takes place on the Piazza di San Pietro, at daybreak. The ceremony is attended by Cardinals in their traditional robes, as well as by the Canons of St. Peter's in their ermine capes. They take their positions near the great brazier—it is of precious metal and of exquisite workmanship, containing in its centre a smaller brazier in a baser metal, in which are ingredients which will burn quickly. Standing in silence, the priests stand waiting for the first sun's ray to appear above the colonnade, which encircles the Piazza. At that moment the fire is lit, a flint being used for the purpose. From this fire are lighted all the lamps and candles of St. Peter's.

When I was a small child it was the custom in private houses to have, in addition to the ordinary open fires, portable braziers, which could be carried from room to room. Ours was a splendid example, worked in brass, and bore the Vitelleschi arms.

After the ceremony of " Benediction of the Fire" on the St. Peter's Piazza, it was the tradition for the people who had tended it, to move to one of the small cafés which lie near by, and there take the customary Easter Saturday hot chocolate and sponge biscuits. In England, hot-cross buns on Good Friday ; in Rome, hot chocolate and sponge biscuits on Easter Saturday.

On this occasion no one dreamt of ordering coffee, for that would be doing in Rome that which the Romans *do not do*. Incidentally, Romans also have their " hot-cross buns," which, locally, are called *Maritozzi*.

As I am writing of Holy Week, I also mention that on the Thursday before Easter the Holy Sacrament is placed in its tabernacle in a side chapel, after which the chapel is decorated with beautiful flowers and plants. In Rome, from one year to another, palms and grass are kept in pots in the vaults of the monasteries and churches ; and during the time that they remain there, no daylight is allowed to reach them. By the following Holy Week their original colour has completely gone, leaving them light cream in colour. They are then used for the decorations of the altars of repose of Maundy Thursday. Mingled with the flowers, and other plants they are most effective. It is also the custom during the Holy Week to go up on one's knees the Scala Santa (Holy Staircase) which is in the building opposite the Basilica of St. John Lateran. Tradition has it, that this is the staircase of the palace of Pontius Pilate, which Our Lord ascended. For protection, each step is encased in thick glass. In fact, Holy Week in Rome is a series of religious ceremonies and ancient customs, going back to the early days of Christendom. From Easter Sunday onwards, Roman social gaieties come to life again in full force.

Amongst the many brilliant parties of those days were those of the two American sisters—Mrs. Hurlbert, who lived on one of the floors of the sumptuous palace of Prince Sciarra in the Corso, and Mrs. Lee, who had a most luxurious villa in Piazza dell' Indipendenza.

They had both lived in Rome for years, and had become more Roman than the Romans. Their kindness and hospitality, and the wonderful success of their dinners and parties were well known to all the International society and Diplomatic Corps of that time.

Mrs. Lee's only daughter, who was perfectly beautiful, married the late Lord Grimthorpe. The present Lord Grimthorpe, who was then Ralph Beckett and quite a small child, is her grandson.

A great many of the Roman society marriages of that time, were Anglo-Italian and American-Italian.

My father had always been a very great friend of Emanuele Ruspoli, Principe di Poggio Suasa, who for a long time was Lord Mayor of Rome, and whose wife, still living, was an American lady of great beauty, Miss Curtis. It is his granddaughter, Manuela Dampierre, who married the second son of the ex-King of Spain two years ago. One year Rome's social festivities were greatly enhanced by the official visits, closely followed one after the other, of the German Emperor (William II) and the

King of England (Edward VII). The Kaiser was accompanied by his two sons, the Kronprinz and Eitel Fritz, the latter being extremely handsome and much admired for his good looks. He was much sought after, as a dance partner.

I watched the arrival of the Royal German visitors from the gardens of the Palazzo Colonna, whose marble terrace overlooks the Piazza del Quirinale.

We had been invited by Princess d'Avella, sister-in-law of Prince Colonna, in whose palace she lived with her husband and family, as is the custom in Italy.

These palaces are so spacious, and well divided, that the cadets of the house can easily reside there with their families, without interfering in any way with the others.

The Piazza was crowded with gaily dressed people, the famous horses of Phidias and Praxiteles had never been so heavily mounted with human beings. The golden-coloured sand which had been strewn for the Royal carriages to drive over, was flanked on each side by the smartest cavalry regiments.

We waited, and suddenly the faint cheers of the people grew louder and louder as the procession approached. It was a gorgeous sight to see all those varied coloured uniforms and helmets glittering in the sun.

A few minutes after entering the palace, the royal guests, with our King and Queen, appeared on the balcony. Then there came, indeed, a tumultuous roar.

Who could foresee on that day the forthcoming horrors of 1914 ?

It is interesting to remember that on one of Kaiser Wilhelm's visits to Rome, a most magnificent ball was given in his honour by Prince Alfonso Doria, whose mother, a Talbot, was a daughter of one of the Earls of Shrewsbury. The ball was at the Palazzo Doria, in the Corso, in its world-famed gallery. The footmen were dressed in the picturesque old Doria livery ; and Venetian chandeliers of incalculable value shed their soft light on the elaborate uniforms, glittering tiaras, and many coloured dresses of the men and women guests.

Wilhelm II was so impressed and so delighted that on taking leave he said to his hosts : " I shall never be able to give you, in Unterderlinden, what you have given me here to-night."

At about the same time King Edward VII also visited Rome, but I cannot now remember whether he came before, or after the Kaiser.

Two gala performances of operas were given— one in honour of the King of England, the other for the German Emperor : Verdi's *Rigoletto* and his *Othello*, with Tamagno (baritone) and Marconi (tenor) in the principal rôles. That great singer's daughter, Valentina Marconi, had been at school with me at the convent.

The scenes of these galas at the Teatro Argentina, the Roman State Theatre, was a never-to-be-forgotten spectacle. Princess Colonna, who was the owner of some wonderful jewellery, wore on these occasions the famous " Marie Mancini " emeralds. These fine stones were presented by Cardinal Mazarin to his niece, Marie Mancini, who in 1661 married the Prince Colonna of the day, the emeralds remaining in the family thereafter.

But more impressive than these balls and gala performances which, on the whole, are very similar in every country, were and are the unique receptions given only on very rare occasions in the galleries of the Capitol Museum. Even the most blasé person is stricken dumb with amazement on seeing this sight for the first time. The Sala degli Arazzi (the tapestry room) is lit in such a way, that the soft light brings out the most delicate shadows of those exquisite tapestries.

The light thrown on the priceless statues, shows up the moulding of the figures and the detail of the muscles so that one would almost say they are alive.

If these and similar functions were chiefly and often exclusively for the benefit of " the upper ten thousand," for the general public there was the great spectacle of the Roman Carnival. Unfortunately, at the time of which I am writing, it was no longer the elaborate and magnificent affair which I several times witnessed when I was quite a little girl.

As children, one of our greatest treats was to be invited to the Palazzo Doria or Palazzo Odescalchi to watch the Carnival procession. The procession consisted of a long line of gaily decorated cars, and vehicles of various kinds, each of which represented a particular subject. It was like a glorified Lord Mayor's Show. In addition to all the carriages and cars, the procession consisted of thousands of masqueraders on foot, and mounted men and women. Many of the decorated cars were drawn by oxen and followed by countless people in Arabian and other costumes. The place of honour in this giant cavalcade was reserved, of course, for Prince Carnival, his Princess, and their Court.

Prince and Princess rode in a great red coach, while their attendants followed on horses. The Carnival ended on Shrove Tuesday with the traditional *La Corsa dei Barbari*. The "Barbari," wild horses from the Roman Campagna, were herded on the Piazza di Venezia and driven down the Corso to the Piazza del Popolo. The horses were gaily decorated and the first one to pass the finishing-post was proclaimed the victor. Many years ago now, the drive of the wild horses was prohibited, following a tragic accident in which one of the procession clowns was fatally injured, and several spectators kicked and trampled.

Horses and "Campagna" remind me that one of the favourite occupations after dinner, on warm June nights, was a ride in the Roman Campagna. As soon as possible after dinner, youthful members of society and numerous attachés from the foreign Embassies and Legations met and started out for the open plains. In the bright moonlight, the sea in the distance looked like a lake of molten silver, and on clear nights, every detail of the delightful surrounding country-side could be seen as distinctly as by day.

Since the time of which I am writing, modern inventions and modern ways have brought many changes. There were, of course, no telephones when I was a child, but as most of our friends lived within a short distance of each other, communication at short notice was not difficult. Nearly everyone, that is, of the society to which we belonged, lived in, or close to, the area which lies between the Piazza di Venezia and the Piazza del Popolo, the two big squares which are joined by the Corso. Nearly every family kept at least two footmen, one of whom spent most of his time carrying messages. If Countess X wished to meet Marchesa Y, she sent a footman with a message. The servant waited for the answer and then returned to his mistress. Generally the answer could be had within a short time.

Telephones were not in general use in Rome until after the turn of the century. Indeed, electricity has revolutionised the home. Instead of the electric bells which are now generally installed in houses, we had the old-fashioned bell-ropes. These ropes ended in a broad " fishtail " of damask on which were the family arms. Instead of the wall-papers, which are familiar nowadays, the walls of the reception-rooms were covered with fine damask. If there was more than one drawing-room, each had damask of a different colour ; and so rooms would be known as the " red drawing-room," the " blue drawing-room," etc.

There was no electric light : houses were illuminated with oil-lamps. Large houses would need as many as thirty or forty of these lamps, and there was a special apartment, the camera oscura (that is dark room), where one man was kept constantly occupied cleaning and filling the lamps, and trimming the wicks.

At receptions and on other occasions, the big chandeliers were brought into use. Frequently they were beautiful works of art, in Venetian glass or crystal, and they sometimes held as many as two or three hundred candles. As the candles burned down, a footman would enter with an extinguisher, extinguish the flame of the dying candle, and substitute a fresh one in its place.

Candle-light is very charming, and is flattering to persons, hence the Italian proverb, *Ne donna, ne tela a luce di candela*, which means that one should never judge a woman or linen by candle-light.

During the winter season in Rome a typical form of entertaining was the evening *salon* given by a number of the leading Roman houses. For instance, on Thursday evening, Countess Guendalina della Somaglia, who occupied a lovely villa on the Piazza dell' Independenza, was at home; Tuesday evening was the occasion of Princess Colonna's reception—which was a social gathering attended by literary people, artists, politicians, and diplomats as well as by members of society. It was an occasion for conversation, about interesting topics of the day, and guests having stayed half an hour, or an hour, and having perhaps sampled the liberal buffet which hostesses provided, left—in many cases to attend another *salon* that was being held on the same evening.

One of the best-loved and most notable personalities at these functions was old Conte Greppi—he lived to the patriarchal age of ninety-four—a tall, wiry, active old gentleman, of amazing energy and vitality, who attributed his excellent health to the fact that never in his life had he worn woollen undergarments.

A great annual celebration, in which all classes joined, was the *Festa dello Statuto*, held in June on the anniversary of the Constitution. In the morning there was a big parade of troops on the famous Piazza d'Armi (overlooked by the delightful Monte Mario—to-day the Piazza is built over), which was reviewed by the King. It was a national holiday for the whole of Italy, and throughout the country there were official receptions and patriotic gatherings of many kinds.

The climax of the *Festa dello Statuto*, was the great evening fireworks on the Pincio terrace overlooking the huge Piazza del Popolo, in the centre of which stand a fine fountain and an obelisk. For days beforehand, this terrace was surrounded by a scaffolding, inside which workmen were busily employed, installing all the necessary equipments for this famous evening. This spectacle called *La Girandola* was an elaborate affair which cost a fabulous sum. The name " *Girandola* " by which it was now known, was given to it on the first occasion of its display, by a shout of the populace, packed like sardines in the Piazza del Popolo, when at the end of the spectacle a huge revolving wheel was seen flaming and turning rapidly in a myriad colours in the sky. " *La Girandola, la Girandola,*" they exclaimed (which means in English an object turning rapidly).

What the reader must understand is that, the mind of the Italian is by nature very child-like, and to the peasants this yearly event was not only a show, but meant to them the reality of their country's constitution. They came to Rome in their thousands from the neighbourhood, from the towns on the hills, from the villages and outlying farms. They put by their *soldi* (pennies) from one year to another, in order to be able to view this sight. They arrived in mule carts, on horses, leading their donkeys on which sat their wives and children.

Special stands were erected in the Piazza to accommodate members of the public, who in many cases paid quite high prices for the privilege of attending, while other people, who were lucky enough to have friends occupying the big houses in the Piazza itself, witnessed the scene from one of the windows. The glamorous display invariably ended with portraits in fireworks of the King and Queen. It probably was the finest pyrotechnical sight to be seen anywhere. Its popularity was also due to the fact that the King and Queen were always present. Their Royal box was placed facing the Pincio, and on either side of it were the stands for the Diplomatic Corps and the Government representatives.

On 3rd April, 1906, my father went out as usual for his afternoon ride. At about four o'clock I left my room, and as I entered the hall, I thought I heard a groan coming from outside. I rushed to the front door, opened it, and to my horror I saw my father coming up the stairs very slowly, and doubled up in pain. We put him to bed, applied hot bandages and other simple remedies, and summoned Dr. Marchiafava, my father's doctor and friend. Papa said that he feared that he was suffering from a chill, and the doctor advised him for the time being, to remain in bed, which he did, and he seemed to be quite himself in the evening; so much so, that he told me he expected to be well enough to go to Florence on the following day, for the bi-monthly meeting of the Italian railways, of which he was then President. Papa also dictated to me his speech, and a rough draft of the speech which he was due to make in the Senate two days hence.

After midnight I left him, and went to bed and dreamed, curiously enough, of Papa's funeral. The dream was abruptly interrupted by my maid, who shook me : " Get up ! Get up ! " she said. " The Marchese is dying."

I was only half awake, and at first I failed to grasp what she meant. I turned upon her angrily and reproved her for frightening me, but when I saw her face I realised that something serious had happened, and I rushed to my father's room. His valet reported that a bell had summoned him to his master's room, and that he had found the Marchese with his head resting on the floor, his feet on the bed and his hand clutching the bell-rope. He had lifted him back to bed and made him as comfortable as possible, and sent again for Professor Marchiafava, who arrived soon afterwards. The professor soon discovered that my father's condition was more serious than his patient had led him to believe, and he called the famous surgeon, Gaetano Mazzoni, who also was a great friend of the family. Mazzoni found that Papa had sustained, in some extraordinary way, a serious internal rupture, and that he was dying.

The doctors then told me that, should Papa recover consciousness, either I might go in and see him or send in to him his confessor, Father Bernardo, of whom he was very fond. The Marchese did recover consciousness for a short while, during which time Father Bernardo was with him. Later I went to his room, but he did not recognise me. He was failing fast.

A bulletin was then issued to say that the Marchese was dying, and great numbers of callers, including personal friends and representatives of the various official bodies, arrived in an unceasing stream to make enquiries and express their sorrow.

At six o'clock on the evening of 4th April, 1906, Marchese Francesco Vitelleschi passed away.

My father, as the first Senator to be created in modern Italy, and one of the best-known men in public affairs at the time—he was a man, too, possessing enormous political influence—was one of the most noted men in the Rome of that day. His death was a shock and a loss to the whole country, and, naturally, he received a public funeral, at which detachments of the fighting forces and representatives of the Court, the Senate, the Municipality, and the public bodies were present. In accordance with the Italian custom, the priests and the Cross followed immediately behind the *cortège*—they preceded the chief mourners and the representatives of the Royal Family.

The wreath on the coffin itself was that of Her Majesty Queen Margherita. The funeral service was at the Church of Santa Maria in Campitelli, which was our parish.

A bust of my father was then placed in one of the halls of the Campidoglio with busts of other famous Italians.

A few days later, a groom from the livery stables at which my father kept his horse came to see me, and asked what was to become of it. I then learnt for the first time that on his last ride my father had been thrown, his horse having put its foot in a rabbit-hole and fallen.

Unfortunately, Papa was thrown on to one of those low rough walls with which the peasants mark the boundaries of their property. It was that fall which caused the injury that proved fatal.

It was typical of my father that not wishing to alarm us—or, for that matter, himself—he tried to keep the nature of his injuries secret.

The groom said the horse was badly injured, and

that hopes of its recovery were small. Regretfully, I gave orders for it to be destroyed.

With the loss of my father and friend, life for me began to shape itself anew. I did not realise then to *what extent* it would change. Although he was seventy-nine, he was so virile that I had never faced the fact of his having to leave me, and now it had come so suddenly and unexpectedly.

My mother was by then a complete invalid, and obliged for her health to live in England; she was unable to travel any more such a long distance to Rome. It was my painful duty to wire to her the news of his death, which was a great blow to her.

This was my first personal contact with the sadness and reality of life. It was only then I began to understand how sheltered my life had been.

A week after my father's death, I sent Paulo, who had been his servant for many years and who remained on with me for some time, to the little church of San Venanzio, which was situated not far from the Palazzo Massimo. Papa used frequently to attend services at this church, and I wished the priest to say a Mass for him. Paulo returned with the information that the only time when the priest would be available to read the Mass was half-past seven on the following morning.

I arrived punctually and stood in the empty church. The priest, in his black vestments, began to recite the Mass for the Dead. In those days I regarded death as a terrible thing; to-day I look upon it in a different way. At the *Oremus* (Let us pray), the priest said: "Let us pray for the soul of Stella Vitelleschi, deceased. . . ." A long-drawn whistle of dismay escaped me and reached the

priest's ear, who turned his head in order to discover
what was amiss. In horror-struck voice I hastened
to correct him.

"No, no! I am Stella Vitelleschi, and I am
alive. It is Papa who is dead; his name is Francesco!" The priest looked at me wearily for a
moment over the top of his spectacles.

"*Va bene*—(all right)—not Stella, but Francesco,"
he said, correcting himself, and continued to read the
Mass. I was much relieved, but to make quite sure
that everything would indeed be all right, I crossed
my fingers and counted 1—3—5—7—9—11—13.
Although I was then eighteen, I was in many ways
very young, and held many superstitions. I believed
absolutely in the existence of fairies, and for that
matter I am not quite sure that I do not still believe
in those friendly little beings, whose dwellings are in
the petals of flowers.

I should like to digress for a moment, to mention
an interesting custom which is still preserved by the
Roman Catholic Church of Rome. It concerns the
funeral service of a *Patrizio Romano* (Roman
Patrician) and is a custom which has been in constant
usage since the Middle Ages. They defined a
Patrizio Romano as a nobleman whose family had
been noble for a considerable time—not less than a
hundred years. The present Patrizio Romano are
descendants of those families and, naturally, are able
to show an aristocratic pedigree which goes back
four, five, and more hundred years.

The funeral service for one of these nobles differs
from that of any other rich, or distinguished person,
in that it is extremely simple. The Order of Service
is prescribed by the *More Nobilium* (Customs of

Nobles). The coffin, instead of resting on a cata-falque, as it would at other people's funerals, is placed on the bare floor on the church. It is sur-rounded by a wooden " fender " (about six or eight inches in height), which is covered with plain black felt. At the corners of the coffin are tall, lighted candles. The deceased nobleman's footmen, wearing full livery and holding torch-candles in their hands, stand round the coffin of their late master. The coffin itself is draped with a cloth of gold, on which there is a large black velvet cross. The service is dignified and simple. The custom orginated from the conviction that as the deceased's position, wealth, and honours were so well known—in ancient times they were gained by deeds of valour, or won in battle—he should face his God simply, unadorned, for what he was worth. God knew his value as well as men. There is no necessity to emphasize it, for even his fellow-men knew all about him.

It was my sad duty, only the other day, to attend the funeral of a well-known Patrizio Romano, who was interred after the simple and impressive service which I have just mentioned. He had been my father's old friend—one of his greatest friends, the Duca Mario Grazioli.

My father had appointed five guardians to watch over my affairs until I became of age, one of them being his sister's daughter, Countess Sgariglia.

Papa's other sister had been the Mother-Superior of the Cloister Convent of San Domenico e Sisto, where I used to go as a child. Two things remain in my memory concerning those visits. The convent belonged to a very strict Order and communication with the nuns was by way of a small, dark grilled

1

window in the *parlour*, through which only a vague form of a nun could be seen.

I remember quite distinctly going as a little girl to see my aunt at this convent. I can still see the bare parlour with a big crucifix, which hung on a white wall, and see the two wooden chairs placed in front of the " grille," and I can still feel the rather frightened beats of my heart when I heard the small shutter being drawn back from the grating. Then, whoever brought me to the convent, either my parents or Nana, lifted me up on one of the chairs, and my little face used to be level with my aunt's. I could not discern her features very well, but I could see her large dark eyes, which my father told me had always been noted for their brilliancy. So fascinated was I by them, that I poked my baby finger through the " grille " to try and touch them, as a result of which I was hastily hauled down from my chair.

This convent used also to make very special biscuits which my aunt sent us at Christmas and Easter.

Another of my guardians was Onorato Caetani, Duke of Sermoneta, one of my father's greatest friends. He had married a Miss Wilbraham and lived at the Palazzo Caetani, a beautiful palace in the picturesquely named Via delle Botteghe Oscure (Street of the Dark Shops.)

Duke Mario Grazioli likewise was an old friend of the family.

My fourth guardian was Giuseppe Serafini, who had married Maddalena Vitelleschi, my first cousin, daughter of my uncle, Giulio. Giuseppe's brother, Cardinal Serafini, is to-day very near the Pope, and has a great position in the Vatican.

My chief guardian was the Queen Mother, and I visited the Queen very often at her residence, which she had taken when she became the Dowager, the former Palazzo Boncompagni, which Her Majesty had renamed Palazzo Margherita.

Queen Margherita used to say that I was amongst those who made her laugh, and there were several incidents during these visits which caused her much amusement. One of them was when I told Her Majesty, how a few days after my father's death our chef, Agostino, known to be one of the best in Rome, came to me one morning whilst I was lunching, and with big tears streaming down his face, he informed me, of his despair in having to leave me. I looked at him in astonishment as there had been no thought yet of giving any of the old servants notice, and I said to him : " But, Agostino, there is no question of sending you away immediately." To which he replied, weeping even more copiously than before : " Donna Stella, my young mistress, you don't understand the horror of my fate. Now that for a whole year you will be in deep mourning, there will be no more dinners, no more parties, therefore, no possibility for me of making a lot of money on the kitchen accounts as I did with the dear, beloved Marchese ! Poor me, poor me, and I loved this house so dearly ! " With these final words he seized my hands and literally bathed them with tears.

During the summer months Rome was infested with that most objectionable of insects—fleas. On one occasion, while I was with the Queen, one of these insects settled on my leg. At once, surreptitiously, without giving the matter further thought, I ended its activities with a quick movement of my finger and thumb, and I continued to hold it there—hoping that an opportunity would occur to dispose of it, without attracting the attention of Her Majesty. But Her Majesty was a keen observer.

" Stella, what have you got there between your fingers ? " I explained and told her that I was terrified of losing it. She was highly amused, laughed, and said : " Then drown it at all costs ! " Upon which I got up and plunged it into one of the Venetian flower vases, which was filled with roses and stood on the mosaic table near us.

One of Queen Margherita's valued possessions was a fine white polar bear-skin rug, which had been presented to her by her nephew, the Duca degli Abbruzzi, who had brought it back from his famous Polar Expedition. It was supposed to have been one of the finest specimens ever seen. It lay in the middle of the Queen's drawing-room.

I was taking leave of Her Majesty, making my exit as the Court etiquette prescribed, by walking backwards and curtseying three times, and I had progressed some way when the Queen suddenly exclaimed :

" Stella, the bear ! "

But the warning was too late. I stepped on the bear's head, lost my balance and fell backwards, ending on the floor in an extremely undignified attitude.

After that episode the bear was removed, the Queen remarked that if, perchance, one of the foreign ambassadors were to fall over in the way I had done, it would be anything but a diplomatic occasion !

Soon after this I was saved from a grave accident in a curious manner.

I have always been a strong believer in the supernatural, and in the help and protection which comes to us from sources beyond this world. Many incidents and events, directly or indirectly affecting myself, have further strengthened that belief.

On one occasion, when I had made all arrangements to leave Rome for London, I suddenly awoke at five o'clock on the morning of my planned departure with a curious conviction that I must not travel. And so I turned over and went to sleep again. Instead of going to London, I spent the day with friends, to whom I explained my reasons for not leaving.

They treated the matter as a joke, enjoyed a hearty laugh at my expense, and recommended me not to give way to absurd fancies.

After dinner that night, when the evening papers were brought to us, we read on the front page, printed in heavy type, the news of a terrible railway accident. The Rome–Turin express had crashed head-on with another train.

There was a ghastly list of dead and injured. My friends were stunned and thankful that this great gift of intuition had been given to me.

Soon after my father's death I had moved into a flat, above the one of Countess Sgariglia, taking with me my father's old valet and my personal maid. My cousin possessed a fine country house at Ascoli, which I visited many times ; this valuable property possessed excellent shooting. The Countess, being very religious, left it all to a convent.

As my mother was still in England and too ill to travel, the care of the estate was left entirely in the hands of my guardians. It was a sad day for me when, in 1925, " Repasto " had to be sold.

With my mother's illness, which lasted thirteen years, and increased in intensity month by month, I came to understand the intolerable pain of having to look on at the suffering of somebody one loves and be totally helpless to relieve them in any way. The doctors expressed the opinion that my mother's creeping paralysis had been caused by a severe fall.

In past days in Rome, lifts were not yet usual, and while walking down Professor Sgambati's stairs, after a musical soirée he had given, she had caught her heel in something and fallen on her back. At the time it seemed of no consequence, but a few years later, whilst playing the piano after dinner one evening at Lamington, she suddenly exclaimed: " Oh, my arm ! " and complained of an acute pain. We all thought it was muscular rheumatism, as she had been sitting out in the garden rather late that afternoon.

Alas ! It was the beginning of the end.

My anguish was increased by the vivid memory of what a beautiful, active, intelligent and energetic woman she had been.

Incidents of all kinds concerning her, unfolded themselves before my eyes one after another, amongst which was the following : My mother, as I have already mentioned, amongst her other accomplishments, painted most attractive landscapes in water colours. One of her masters, who taught her the art of softening light and shade, was Roesler Franz, a great aquarellist in Rome at the time, and also a friend. One afternoon in December Mama went off by herself with her camp-stool, paint-box, and brushes. When my father came home at seven-thirty that evening from the Senate, his valet told him that the household was very alarmed, as the Marchesa had not yet returned. He added that she had gone out on foot, with her painting things, without saying where she was going.

In those days there were no telephones, so one could not ring up friend after friend to know if she were there.

My father, who was then " Assessore Municipale " —a big position at the Capitol which corresponds to the Mansion House in London—sent one footman to the Capitol, and the other to the Chief of Police. Within an hour my father, with ten policemen and twenty Municipal Guards, started scouring, with torches, the ancient gardens and other places of interest where she might have gone to paint. My father was distracted ; he feared all kinds of accidents had happened to her. In time they reached the Forum, descended amongst the ruins, and searched for her in every possible and impossible spot, whilst my father went on calling her by name : " Amy ! Amy ! "

They suddenly heard a faint cry ; it came from their right, where stood the Palatine gardens and the ruins of the palaces of the Cæsars. The searchers at once rushed there, and, as the torches blazed in the night, it might have reminded one of the race of the torch-bearers.

The closed gates were forced open and, on arriving at the top terrace of the Palatine, they found Mama, who, having gone there to paint a Roman twilight, had become so engrossed in her work that she completely forgot the time and got locked in. The guardian never suspected the presence of anybody in that remote part of the gardens, and being a dark night, she could not find her way down to the gates.

She was always outwardly very calm, but showed much relief at seeing the rescue party, and turning to my father with that charming smile of hers, which always attracted everyone, she said: "*Tant de torches pour une frêle petite femme*" (So many torches for a frail, small woman). She added that her only worry had been that her absence was causing anxiety.

The procession walked through the ruins which, for the first time since their past splendour were being lit up at night.

It was eleven o'clock when my parents got back to Palazzo Massimo.

In those days I used to go to bed at 6.30, therefore, I knew nothing of all this until the next morning when, as usual, I scrambled on to the foot of my mother's bed whilst she had her breakfast.

My favourite pastime on these mornings used to be to look at some albums belonging to her. These albums are most original, and I often look at them even now with delight.

When my mother was a little girl of eleven, she used to cut out the photographs of the various people she, and her family knew, paste them into these albums, and then draw and paint various scenes around them. For instance, on one page she stuck the photograph of my Aunt Violet, who was then also a little girl (now Violet, Viscountess Melville) in bed ill; in the centre of the room a table literally covered with medicine bottles, and my grandmother seated by the bedside holding her daughter's hand.

Still another memory comes to me as I write. My

father could never resist telling this little story, although really the joke was against himself : my parents at the time were staying for a few days at Fogliano, the very picturesque country seat of the Caetani. One afternoon my father took my mother out for a drive in the dogcart ; it was one of the small ones which were used in Italy. One person sat in front driving, and the other behind. A vivid conversation was going on between them of some matter of interest, and Papa was pouring forth his opinions, and ended up by saying : " Isn't that your idea also ? " No reply. Thinking she had not quite grasped what he said, he added : " Because to be more explicit, what I mean is . . . " and he went on into more detail concerning his argument. Still no reply. He then turned round and, to his dismay, was greeted by an empty seat ! No trace of his wife. He instantly understood that she must have slipped off. Quickly he drove back and, before he had gone very far, he saw Mama sitting quietly on a heap of stones at the side of the road !

But to return to the sad fact of my father's death : The Guardianship of the Five proved very soon to be an exceedingly inconvenient arrangement. Every decision taken had to receive the assent of the Five, and five signatures were needed for each document relating to the estate. Often in this way delay occurred before important matters of business were settled.

I continued to spend the summers in England and the winters in Rome, where I retained the same flat until Countess Sgariglia left. I then moved close to my very great friends, Signor and Signora Allievi, whose daughter, Fanny, had been at the convent with me. The Allievis were like a father and mother to me, and Fanny a loving sister, and the time I spent with them passed very happily.

On 28th December, 1908, at two o'clock in the morning, there occurred one of the most hideous and appalling calamities that Europe has ever witnessed. I refer to the earthquake at Messina, in Sicily, that ill-fated island in the sunny Mediterranean, which already had enough troubles of its own. It was the home and happy hunting-grounds of that evil secret society, the Mafia, who reached the peak of their activities about 1860-70, but who continued their reign of terror until only a few years ago. In 1928 these robbers, smugglers, and murderers were finally stamped out by decree of Signor Mussolini, who dispatched Cesare Mori on a special mission to the Island. As Prefect of Sicily, Cesare Mori ruthlessly exterminated them. It is said that those of the old Mafia who succeeded in escaping from Sicily, now form the backbone of the American gangster scum.

At the time of the earthquake, a strong wave of atheism was passing over Italy, and there were public demonstrations against the Church. On Christmas Eve it is the custom in Roman Catholic churches to hold midnight Mass and Communion. Also, in the cathedral of Messina there was midnight celebration. After Mass, among others, about twenty students went to the altar to receive Communion. They took the Communion wafers from the officiating priest. At a given signal they spat out the wafers, and, standing up, shouted in unison : " If there is a Christ, may we be destroyed within a week ! "

The priest began a prayer : " May God forgive

this blasphemy, and have mercy upon these poor sinners. . . ." He attempted to gather up the remnants of the wafers.

Three days later Messina was visited by a fearful earthquake, which was followed by a tidal wave. There was a huge death-roll and the city and surrounding places were reduced to ruins. Thousands were rendered homeless. Rescue work was extremely difficult.

Eventually, the homeless, the injured, and the orphans were evacuated ; and for the time being they were given shelter in Italian cities and towns—particularly in Rome. Many people temporarily vacated their houses and flung them open to the refugees. A very great friend, Donna Bice Marotti, turned her beautiful villa into a home for infant refugees, who either had been rendered orphans or who had become separated from their parents. Donna Bice asked another friend, Fanny Allievi, and myself to give our services during the daytime, and help to nurse the children.

" Will you look after this little girl ? " asked Donna Bice, placing in my arms a small infant of about six months. She was a delightful baby, and a medal on a small chain which hung round her neck gave her name as Assunta. I took charge of her. The doctor attached to the home instructed me to prepare a small bath of warm oil. When I had done this, he gave me an ivory paper-knife and told me to very gently scrape the child's body, which was literally caked with dirt ; in fact, it was quite obvious that she had never been washed since her birth. This was no easy task I had been given ; it was truly a Lenten penance, and the baby did not make matters easier, for she kicked and screamed, which made her very difficult to hold, as she continually slipped from my hands, and I was somewhat nervous that she would be drowned in olive oil !

However, by the third day she quite enjoyed her daily bath, but to get her *quite* clean it took five days ! Where the dirt had eaten its way into the skin, little white scars were left. In the course of time I became attached to " my " little girl, who turned out to be a very lovable little creature.

We had posted outside the villa a notice board, giving particulars of the inmates of the crèche, in the hope that some of their fathers and mothers would arrive and claim them. One day I was told that a man had come to claim little Assunta. I carried her down into the hall. I saw a tall, black-moustached, fierce-looking Sicilian—Assunta's father. When he stooped to look at his infant daughter he refused to believe she was his. Drawing himself up, a torrent of abuse poured from his lips. He swore that the child had been ruined by our cleaning her, and he cursed us all. I said we had given the child every attention. For a reply he struck me, causing me to reel backwards, and I almost fell on the stairs, still clasping the baby in my arms. Hearing all this noise, the hall soon filled with people who came to my rescue and overpowered the enraged father. The Sicilian resolutely refused to take the child unless we returned her to him in the same state she was in, when she arrived. This, of course, was impossible, so poor little Assunta was delivered over to an orphanage.

Following the terrible earthquake, the Press, which had published reports of the blasphemous scene in the Cathedral, attributed it to the vengeance of God.

Its chief effect was that atheism, which had begun to grow, lost ground and eventually faded away.

Unhappily, the paralysis from which my mother was suffering had grown more serious, and instead of going to Scotland for the summer months she decided to take a small house and garden near Winchester, where it was intended that I should join her at the beginning of May, 1913. A change of tenants at our property, Repasto, made it necessary for me to postpone my departure for England for about a fortnight. I write to my mother telling her this, and also to her doctor, who replied that, organically, there was no cause for alarm concerning Mother's health and that in all probability she would live for many years longer.

A few days after the receipt of that letter, an old friend came to see me, and we became engrossed in a conversation, during the course of which she asked me to do her the favour of mentioning something to Queen Margherita. We then proceeded to discuss the " something." At three o'clock exactly—I clearly remember the hour—for no obvious reason I suddenly clutched my head and broke out into a fit of sobbing.

" Mama is dead ! " I exclaimed.

My friend, who was considerably older than myself, reasoned with me, shook me, and endeavoured to persuade me " not to give way to such weakness," as she described it. But I was convinced of the truth of my conviction and told my friend that I intended to pack at once and leave for England. Nothing that she said was able to change that resolve. When

I went downstairs, on my way to catch the evening train, I met a telegraph messenger-boy on his way up.

"It's a telegram for Vitelleschi," I said to him. As I had expected, it was a message for me. Without stopping to open it, I continued to the station and took my place in the train. When we had left Rome behind, I opened the telegram, which contained the following message from my Aunt Violet:

"Mother passed away quietly to-day at three o'clock—Aunt Violet."

CHAPTER VII

MY SECRET MARRIAGE—MY SON'S BIRTH

MY last chapter ended on a somewhat sad note, so I shall, anyway, begin this one with some amusing incidents!

The Roman season goes on, year after year, as the London one does here, like a kaleidoscope of people coming and going. It was during one of these seasons that the following episode happened, and, incidentally, gave me scope for one of the best bits of acting I have ever done. Sir Rennell Rodd (now Lord Rennell of Rodd) was then the British Ambassador in Rome, and Lady Rodd, a most beautiful and talented woman, was a great friend of my family. She always tried to think of some new ideas to enliven the entertainments of the Embassy receptions—which, naturally, are inclined to be somewhat of a sameness. A few days before one of these parties a brilliant idea struck her, and she sent for me at once and unfolded her plan. The result of our confabulation was that on the evening of the reception I arrived at the Embassy at six o'clock, and was shown straight up to Lady Rodd's bedroom. After an hour's preparation, there emerged from the room a most attractive, fascinating woman with golden hair, dressed in the latest fashion and encircled by a sparkling diadem; she was exceedingly well made up, and her green and gold lamé dress, just arrived from Paris, was enhanced by her jewellery ; she carried in her hand lorgnettes hanging from a diamond chain. When the house-party had assembled for dinner, and had been introduced to the Comtesse de Solanges, dinner was announced ; Sir Rennell turned to his wife and said : " I thought Stella was coming to dinner."

" No, she is coming after," was Lady Rodd's reply.

Dinner went off merrily, and the Comtesse was the spirit of the party, expressing freely her opinions on every subject.

The official reception commenced at ten o'clock, and crowds began streaming into the spacious drawing-room where rows of gilded chairs were arranged to view the *tableaux vivants* which Lady Rodd had announced. Everybody knew that anything that Lady Rodd arranged was sure to be a success, so full of artistry, knowledge, and imagination was she.

Our friends in Rome still speak to-day of the marvellous spectacle of the Grecian dances, held in the Embassy gardens one afternoon in June, which gave one the illusion of being transported to the Athens of the past.

Not only did Lady Rodd plan, but she carried her ideas out, and worked at every little detail herself with indefatigable energy. She was indeed the spirit of inspiration. But to return to our " Comtesse."

By the end of the *tableaux*, the rumour had got round that the Comtesse de Solanges was a very rich young widow and would not be averse to a second marriage. She was soon surrounded by many men, young and old, who had asked to be introduced to her. Appointments were made for the following days at her suite at the Grand Hotel! Alas! when these gentlemen called, one after the other, they were told that no such person lived at the hotel; so amazed were some of them, that they enquired of Lady Rodd whether they had made a mistake concerning the name of the hotel. And then the truth came out!

Stella Vitelleschi had been, for a few hours, the alluring Comtesse de Solanges!

During the summer of 1913 I stayed for some time at Sandbeck Park, the country home of my cousins the Earl and Countess of Scarborough, and in the evenings I was often called upon, to perform a number of improvised monologues for the amusement of my hosts and their guests. Of the latter, two who were a great deal in the public eye at the time, were Sir George Goldie, of Nigerian fame, and Lord Claud Hamilton.

The question of my future career came up during this visit and my histrionic talent as an amateur led to the stage being suggested—and no profession could have been more to my fancy. Actually, unknown to the family, I had already acted on this suggestion, and, equipped with a letter of introduction to Sir George Alexander, went to see him. This letter was penned by Alice Nory, who had been on the Paris stage and who, on George Alexander's invitation, had come to London to act at the St. James's Theatre. She was the daughter of Berthe Carter, who in 1870 had fled from Paris from the advancing Germans, then becoming the governess to my mother and my Aunt Violet (Viscountess Melville).

K

When I told Sir George that I wished to become an actress he asked : " Are you just another of these society girls whose object is to seek diversion for a few weeks or months, or do you seriously mean to make it your profession, and are you willing to start from the bottom ? "

I said that I was serious about it and that it was my wish to start at the very beginning and progress by merit.

" Very well," he said, " then I'll let you ' walk on ' in my play, *Turandot*, here at the St. James's."

Without hesitation I accepted the offer and received a salary of one guinea a week, from which the sum of threepence was deducted for a stamp, which caused me much amusement. We then fell to discussing a stage name for myself, as out of consideration for my relations—as one or two of them were opposed to my becoming an actress—I could not perform under my own name. Several " possibles " were suggested, but we were unable to decided upon any of them. It was then that another caller was announced.

" Here's the author himself," said George Alexander. " Let's see if he has any ideas."

Turning round I saw Carl Vollmoeller, Reinhardt's right hand : " Carlo ! " I cried out, and ran to meet him.

" Why, Stella," he said, " I haven't seen you for years."

Carl had married a very great friend of mine, Norina Gilli, who, as Maria Carmi, was in London acting the part of the Madonna in Reinhardt's great spectacle, *The Miracle*, at Olympia. As I had not seen her for a long time, and we never wrote to each other, I was not aware that she was in England, still less did I dream she had gone on the stage.

This unexpected meeting reminded George Alexander that Carl's wife had at one time intended acting under the stage name of " Maria Rho," but when enquiries were made it was discovered that a long while ago there had been an actress of that name. And so she became " Maria Carmi."

" The solution is a simple one," said Sir George. " We'll call you ' Stella Rho.' "

And that was how I came to receive my stage name.

Incidentally, at the St. James's Theatre I was known as the " Codfish," as Rho soon became pronounced " roe."

Following my reunion with Carl Vollmoeller, I naturally went to see Maria Carmi, who was thrilled at hearing that I, too, was following her example. I used often to go and see her beautiful performance at Òlympia, and I am sure that any person who saw it then will never forget it. One of the reasons why it was so impressively real was, I think, because of the immense space the spectacle spread over. I was told that some of the actors, during each performance, walked two miles.

The beginnings of my career at the St. James's Theatre, are amongst some of my happiest memories.

Sir George's consideration and kindness for all those who worked under him made him the most loved manager ; his staff used to grow old in his service. The St. James's Theatre was really like a home of a big, happy family to all those who entered it.

Every evening before the curtain went up, Lady Alexander used to come round on a tour of inspection, and ask every one of us without exception, if we were all right and had all we wanted; and her keen eye would detect any little defect in the dressing-rooms. She never failed us, even though she might be going out to some dinner or reception.

Even my friends and relations who agreed to my taking up the stage as a career, all thought it far better to keep it from my grandmother, as in her young days such things were not done.

I had not long been associated with *Turandot*, when my grandmother asked me on a certain evening to accompany her to the St. James's! It was an awkward moment, but I had the presence of mind to plead a previous engagement, and grand-mamma went without me. I "went on" as usual, trembling lest she should see me, but luckily she never recognised me.

When *Turandot* ended I paid a short visit to Rome and on my way there I stopped as usual in Paris. Achille Trombetti and another friend of mine were there also, and they used to take me out in the evenings. One day they told me that they had been instructed to go and visit one particular apache den, disguising themselves as apaches, to find out how many Italians were also linked up with the gang. They asked me whether it would interest me to go with them, in which case I, too, should have completely to disguise my identity. I was thrilled at the idea, and naturally answered in the affirmative.

I could not, of course, leave the hotel in my get-up, so it was arranged that I should go and dress in a small out-of-the-way room which they had hired for the purpose. When I arrived, they were already dressed, and I hardly recognised them; they looked like two awful tramps. While I was dressing they waited for me at the " bistro "—which is a sort of public house. When I looked at myself in the mirror, before joining them, the whole of my personality seemed entirely changed.

The three of us started for our destination, walking through narrow, dimly lit streets. On reaching a tumbledown door, Trombetti knocked in a certain way and a frightening face appeared. After an exchange of words, evidently pass-words, the man let us in, and led us down a winding stair, by the aid of a candle, and finally we reached a door which admitted us to a cellar—a bare place containing a miserable piano and a few primitive tables and chairs. In one corner there was a rustic counter, on which were sausages, rolls, beer, and other simple foods and beverages.

We sat at one of the long tables and listened to a man playing the piano and singing a number of songs. To our surprise, a sad tone ran through all of them. One was the lament of a mother weeping over her dead baby. The other a broken-hearted father weeping over his son who had been killed by the police. Strange to relate, not one of their songs was coarse or obscene.

After a little while, a poorly dressed, youngish woman came in, looking anxiously round, and then went towards a man seated at one of the tables. The apache turned round to her :

" What have you got ? " he asked roughly. The woman showed a watch and chain, some notes of small value and a few coins—all she had been able to bring in, and which she had hidden in her bodice. Her man immediately jumped up, struck her a vicious blow, and knocked her down. He then proceeded to kick her savagely in the stomach until I feared that he would kill her. Having administered the most terrible punishment, the apache then—to my amazement—knelt down on the floor at her side, took her in his arms, and showed a tenderness that I would not have believed possible. They remained there for a considerable time, she weeping and he consoling her. He seemed full of contrition for what he had done.

Some time after this episode, while we were eating sausages and drinking beer, one of the men sitting opposite us asked Trombetti :

" Are you going to Marseilles to-morrow ? "

Trombetti said that he was, whereupon the other suggested that he should first visit a certain individual whom they called " Jean." Trombetti asked for his address.

" Have you a pencil ? " asked the man.

No one had a pencil.

" All right—that doesn't matter," he answered.

Then, to our horror, he produced from his pocket a sheath-knife, made an incision in the third finger of his right hand, bound a handkerchief round the lower part of the said finger and in his own blood wrote the address on a dirty piece of paper which he produced from his pocket. If Trombetti had not ground his heel on my foot, until I was almost ready to shout with pain, I should certainly have fainted.

Trombetti pocketed this gruesome souvenir, and after a few minutes he suggested in a nonchalant way that it was time for us to go.

Once clear of that neighbourhood we returned to our " dressing-room " and, one after the other, donned our own clothes. I must confess that although I was most interested in all I had seen, and would not have missed it for the world, I was glad to get into a taxi with my two friends who took me to the Café de la Paix, where we ended our night by drinking champagne, and after eating a good supper I was more than happy to get back to my nice clean room at the Hotel Splendid where I was then staying.

Two days later I went to Rome, where, as usual, I stayed the winter.

The only excitement that happened to me during those months was a motor accident, which, for the second time, nearly sent me into the next world.

Some alterations had to be made to the farmhouse at Repasto, and my lawyer suggested driving me down there, as the scenery on the way is very beautiful and he thought I would enjoy it. His car was an open touring Fiat. We had been driving for some miles when we came to a bend in the road where there was a bridge over a small stream. I had a sudden feeling that we should hit the bridge, and it flashed through my brain that my one chance of salvation was to relax my whole body. The crash was terrific, and I felt myself soaring through the air, then suddenly I hit the ground and sank on my hands and knees into something soft. It seemed hours to me before I heard the lawyer calling out in desperate tones: "Where are you? Where are you?" This question seemed to me particularly stupid, as quite obviously, I thought, I must be near the car and therefore quite visible. As he continued to call, I slowly raised my head, and in doing so, struck it against the trunk of a big tree which was within an inch of where I had fallen. I picked myself up, and looked with wonder around me. I was in a big orchard, which had not been apparent from the road we had been on. I really felt like Alice in Wonderland, except that I had a most excruciating pain in my left knee.

My lawyer's voice calling to me became more and more desperate. This time I answered and said: "Where are you? I don't know where I am." I walked down the incline, following the sound of his voice, and then I saw what had happened. I had been flung over a tall bank and hedge about 16 feet high and had landed in the orchard.

Happily it had rained a lot, and the ground was very soft, so I sank as I fell.

I always put down my escape to a little medal which hung round my neck, and had only been given to me the day before.

The car was broken to pieces, and the bridge badly damaged.

We had to walk two miles before reaching Terni, where we got a train back to Rome.

By the time I arrived home my knee had swollen very much, and it was some days before it was all right.

Ten days later I left for England.

As usual, I took my sleeper from Rome, and installed myself comfortably for a nice night's rest; for the extraordinary thing is, that I sleep better in a train than anywhere else. In fact it is a treat to me to travel by night, and I always look forward to it.

About half an hour after I had got into my bunk, my nose started bleeding violently. Handkerchiefs, towels, pillow-case were completely soaked; at last it stopped. Not knowing what to do with these blood-stained articles, I took a piece of string out of my pocket (of which my pockets are always full !) made a clothes' line from the window to the top of my bunk, hung all the things on, turned over and went to sleep. I was half awakened by murmurs outside my door, and strange words such as " doctor . . . accident . . . alone . . . suicide . . ." reached my ears. Most annoyed at being wakened up, I pulled the sheet well over my head, and politely wished them further ; but, alas, my wish was not to be granted ! My door was flung open, all the lights turned on, and I saw three men were staring at me— the conductor, the guard, and a third who turned out to be a doctor. On seeing me in perfect health, they were somewhat taken aback. They then explained that, when I was sound asleep, the conductor had passed by to ask at what time I wanted to be called in the morning ; seeing all these blood-stained garments, he thought some dreadful tragedy had happened—and he had rushed to get help !

The doctor spoke to me for a few minutes and told me that, in his opinion, this violent hæmorrhage of the nose had been caused by the shock of my accident, and the movement of the train had released the congestion.

I was staying two or three days in Paris, as usual, with my friends Alice Nory and her mother, Berthe Carter.

On arriving at the Gare de Lyon the porter was putting my luggage in a taxi when my eyes caught sight of an enormous scaffolding which had been erected where previously some old houses had stood. This scaffolding was plastered with various posters and advertisements ; the one which seemed specially intended for my benefit (after my nose treating me so badly !) was the following :

" Pourquoi s'entêter à vivre, lorsqu' on peut mourir et être enterré comfortablement pour 75 frs.
S'adresser à..............................."

(Why insist on living when you can die and be comfortably buried for 75 frs. Refer to...........
and then followed the name and address of the undertakers !)

How things have changed ; death has become much more an *affaire de luxe* in these days !

I spent a happy time with my friends and I arrived in London without further mishap.

As far as the general public were concerned, nothing seemed more remote than the possibility of war. The London Season was at its height ; people were happily planning their holidays ; the weather was ideal, and it seemed that nothing could intervene to mar the gaiety which was apparent everywhere.

I remember one evening at a dinner-party making a terrible *faux pas* without realising it, and what hilarity it caused. My hostess was telling of a splendid solicitor who lived next door to her, and who was well known for divorce cases, his clients being generally women. She added that he gave wonderful parties to which many of these ladies were invited : " So," she said, " if any of you have one day need of his services, you will know where to go ! " " Oh, I see," was my reply, " he gives parties for women soliciting ! "

Everyone was convulsed, and I could not understand what was causing their mirth until they explained the joke. This little incident shows how similar words have quite different meanings in different languages ; and although one may speak two or three of them fluently, one may sometimes make a mistake.

Soon, alas, August arrived, and with it the beginning of four years of horror, suffering, and destruction, in the most terrible war the world has yet experienced.

My English relations strongly advised me to abandon my intention of returning to Rome for the winter, as the war had now extended over the whole of Central Europe, and as there seemed to be a great possibility that sooner or later Italy would also become involved. And so, following their advice, I took my mother's furniture from the warehouse in which it had been stored, and removed it to a small flat at St. Andrew's Mansions in Dorset Street. I decided upon these flats because they were equipped with an open iron staircase and balconies where, in summer, baskets of red geraniums were hung. They reminded me constantly of Italy.

At a big tea-party once, various friends of mine started teasing me about my abode, saying I lived in tenement flats. His Royal Highness Philippe, Duc d'Orleans, who was also one of the guests, overheard it, and full of amused curiosity asked details about it, and expressed the wish to come and see it, and so the following day he walked up the three floors of iron staircase to have tea with me. He had been a great friend of my parents and we talked a lot about many of our mutual friends.

The little home was shared by my loyal Italian maid, Ersilia, who remained with me in London for six years. During the whole of that time she obstinately and resolutely declined to learn English, but on the other hand imparted a smattering of Italian to large numbers of the local tradespeople. The milkman would arrive in the morning and in a very English accent exclaim : " *Latte, latte !* " (milk).

At this time my future husband, Achille Trombetti, had come to London to perfect his English as he was going to enter the Italian diplomatic service, and he told me all about a fellow-countryman, Angelo Cucchiara by name, who had founded in the years immediately preceding the war, a great organisation called " Cosmopolis." It covered many activities. In one department there was a travel and ticket bureau ; another department acted as an authors' and artists' agent ; and yet another acted as a sort of Universal Aunt. At the Association's head-quarters at 201 High Holborn there was an excellent club, and—the thing which principally interested me—an admirably conducted theatre.

The theatre was international and plays were produced and acted by the French, Italian, German and other sections in turn. This new venture became so popular that within a few months of its opening, the Association had no fewer than ten thousand members.

One of the most distinguished patrons of Cosmopolis was Princess Alice of Monaco. Regularly for many years the Princess spent several months at Claridge's in London where she held numerous receptions. The Princess's " drawing-room " was attended by members of international society, by representatives of the Diplomatic Corps as well as by authors, artists, and interesting personalities of the day. I became a friend of Her Highness, and soon it was taken for granted that I lunched with her every Sunday. On those occasions I had many chances of observing the luxury and studied comfort with which she liked to surround herself.

Princess Alice, who was fabulously wealthy, was a woman of culture, refinement, admirable good taste, and she possessed that remarkable knack—it is not often possessed by rich persons—of not only sympathising with the poor, but of instinctively understanding exactly their needs.

Once a week the Princess, wearing a suit of plain clothes, which she reserved specially for the purpose, left Claridge's by car, surrounded with an enormous number of parcels and armed with a list that was supplied to her by the French Consulate. The list contained the names and addresses of poor French inhabitants of some of the most wretched slums that are to be found in the Metropolis. She drove to these homes of poverty and left at each of them precisely those things of which the people were most in need—blankets, provisions, shoes, clothes, etc. In addition, she left at each home the sum of one pound. The filth and horror and misery of some of those homes were incredible ; many of them were little better than pigsties.

But neither by word nor by gesture did the Princess give any indication of the disgust and horror which she must have felt : her kindness and tact merited the highest admiration. I am able, personally, to testify this, as on various occasions, at her invitation, I accompanied her on these errands of mercy.

The Princess owned near Chartres in France a delightful property by the name of Hauts Buissons.

I was invited, and stayed there for a week in the summer. After life in London it was like being in fairyland There is no need for me to mention that the furniture and appointments of the house were the last word in luxury, but the " extra " equipment certainly was rather surprising. The bathrooms, as big as churches almost, were furnished with every conceivable, and inconceivable, appliance ; one tap dispensed eau-de-Cologne. In the bedrooms, beside the bed, there was a kind of switchboard with a number of operating buttons, each of which was named. There was a button which opened and closed the door ; another locked it ; yet another opened and closed the window. And there were buttons for summoning the lady's maid and the butler. Post Office telephones were in every room. No guest was allowed to buy his own stamps or pay for his own telegrams, an arrangement having been made with the postal authorities for all such to be charged to the Princess. Nor would she permit guests to give tips to the servants ; while at her house they were not allowed to incur any expenses whatsoever. The Princess kept a little book in which she recorded the name of the guest and the dates of his arrival and departure. *She* then paid the tips in accordance with the length of the stay.

My first introduction to Cosmopolis had been in connection with the popular play *La Cena delle Beffe*, by Sem Benelli—its English title was *The Jest*.

One evening whilst dining at the Trocadero restaurant with Trombetti, he told me that he was tired out, having run about all day for Cucchiara, to try and find someone adequate to play the part of " Giannetto." They had searched in the Italian quarter, they had asked at the Italian school, and even at the Italian hospital, but all in vain. I must explain that the part of " Giannetto " (like the one of " Cherubin " in the play of *Beaumarchais*) is generally played by a woman, as the Latin youth of sixteen would be too incompetent to handle these difficult parts, and an older man would not be appropriate. Trombetti mentioned that Cucchiara was so desperate to get somebody that he was offering a hundred pounds to anybody who could do it. I jumped up, and said excitedly : " Pay the bill, we'll go straight to Cosmopolis, and I'll play the part ! " He murmured something about there being no need to hurry as we had not finished our dinner, but I listened to nothing and off we went. On arriving at Cosmopolis I was introduced to Cucchiara, an extremely pleasant-looking man, who was sitting at a table in the little restaurant downstairs. He appeared the picture of misery. Three other men were with him, and on our entrance they turned to look at us, and they asked Trombetti anxiously if he had been successful in finding somebody.

" Yes, he has found me ! I am going to play it ! " I said.

They stared at me dumbfounded. " You, Signora ? " replied Cucchiara.

" Yes, of course," quickly came my answer, and added : " I am so certain of the success I shall achieve, that I make you the sporting offer that if I am a failure, you don't pay me the hundred pounds ! "

Cheerful faces and drinks of vermouth ended this meeting.

We started rehearsals next day, which progressed feverishly as we had only a fortnight before the play.

We could only rehearse three hours in the evenings after dinner, as most of the artists were people who worked during the day. The great night came and I must say that *La Cena delle Beffe* was a tremendous success, and congratulations poured in on every side, and I was told that I was the making of the play. Needless to say, the hundred pounds were mine.

One of the performances was witnessed by no less a judge than Sir Herbert Tree, who afterwards paid me a very handsome compliment. Sir Herbert, in fact, so liked my acting that he held out to me a promise that, should the opportunity occur, he would like me to take part in the production of this play at His Majesty's, and to play the same rôle in the English version of Arthur Symons. Unhappily this was prevented by Sir Herbert's death. The part of "Giannetto" had been played in the French version by Sarah Bernhardt in Paris.

I continued with Cosmopolis and became head of the Italian section, which produced many of the d'Annunzio plays as well as the lighter works of Bracco.

Meanwhile, Achille Trombetti constituted himself my A.D.C. and stage manager at "Cosmopolis," and we became great companions.

All this time the war was growing in extent and gravity, and in May, 1915, Italy decided to throw in her lot with the Allies. That marked the beginning of the end of Cosmopolis, for there were no men left to fill the masculine rôles. Those who only a short while ago had been such good friends and loyal comrades on our little London stage, were soon to be fighting and slaying each other on the battle-fields of Europe. And the one living memory of Cosmopolis

By Percival Anderson

THE AUTHOR

in London is now in Knightsbridge, in the Beautiful Venetian glass shop of which Angelo Cucchiara is the manager. Often do I go in and talk to him of our past happy days and glories.

It was during this same year 1915 that Rejane organised the wonderful Allied Woman's Matinée for the Red Cross, at the Haymarket Theatre. The leading actresses of all the allied countries were to take part. Eleonora Duse was to represent Italy. Four days before the matinée took place, a wire from Duse and her doctor informed Rejane that it was quite impossible for her to come from Italy as she was laid up with bronchitis. I had had the privilege of knowing Rejane for some time, and she was very fond of me and had great faith in me.

" Stella," she said, " I am going to give you your chance. You shall take Duse's place. Learn d'Annunzio's poem on Victory and come and rehearse it for me on the Haymarket stage at eleven on the morning of our matinée."

I arrived punctually, the stage was littered with benches and flower-pots and plants which the stage hands were putting in their proper places for the afternoon. Rejane went up to the dress circle; I stood in the middle of the stage and recited my Italian poem.

" Translate it into French now, verse by verse, so that I understand every word," said Rejane when I had finished. I did so. The poem is the one out of d'Annunzio's *Laudi*, describing the man walking alone on a dusty road, then hearing suddenly the noise of horses and chariots galloping behind him, coming nearer and nearer to him, passing him, and dashing towards the glorious sun of Victory. Rejane listened to me, and then explained to me in the most vivid way how I must see, and hear, and feel, in my own brain every word I am saying, in order to convey the reality of that description to the audience.

" To convey a feeling to others you must first and foremost feel it yourself," said Rejane.

In that one hour she taught me the greatest lesson in acting.

I was very nervous at the matinée whilst waiting for my turn ; when it came, Rejane took me by the hand, led me to the centre of the stage, read out Duse's telegrams to the audience, smiled at me and said : " Courage, *petite etoile.*"

I followed her teachings. I was so engulfed in what I was saying that I really felt that there were horses and chariots around me. I entirely forgot where I was. The clamorous applause of the public brought me back to reality. I owe a great deal to Rejane ; I have a very nice photograph of her which she gave me in souvenir of this matinée, and it is most dear to me.

When I started my stage career I began to know various interesting dramatic authors of the day. Often I used to go and dine with Haddon Chambers in his delightful house at Mount Street. He was a very great friend of my cousin, Gilbert Earl de la Warr ; Louis N. Parker also had great faith in me as a dramatic actress, he used to speak very good Italian and many an hour I used to spend talking to him in his Kensington study across his huge horse-shoe desk.

Trombetti, who had returned to Rome to sit for the examinations at the Ministry of Foreign Affairs, passed them with flying colours, being first out of ninety-seven candidates, and he was appointed secretary to the Italian Embassy in St. Petersburg, where Marchese Carlotti was Ambassador.

I was feeling very depressed and lonely at this time and Trombetti asked me if he might call to say good-bye on the morning of his departure from London for Russia. He came at half-past nine and produced from his breast pocket a special licence. He then pleaded to be allowed to become my legal protector, no matter where he might be during those terrible days of war. I knew that he had been in love with me for a number of years and, without giving myself time to consider all the aspects of his proposal, I consented.

So we rushed to the Marylebone Registry Office, where we married, our witnesses being an old woman who was selling apples and a butcher's boy, who left his bicycle leaning against a wall. On conclusion of the civil ceremony we dashed to St. James's Church, Spanish Place. I then said good-bye to my husband, who jumped into a taxi and left for his appointment in Russia.

At that time the censorship between that country and England was very severe, and all correspondence was practically impossible.

A year passed. A year of anxiety and worry, wondering if I should ever see him again.

In 1915 Doris Keane produced *Romance* at the Duke of York's Theatre. It failed miserably. But Miss Keane had faith in her play and, with her manager, Louis Nethersole (brother of Olga), she decided to risk a big gamble and to transfer, with a great flourish of trumpets, to the Lyric. Hundreds of sandwich-men paraded London with the well-known portrait of Doris Keane in her long black dress of the second act and her big string of pearls. The play was boomed and advertised by every means available. On the opening night the theatre was besieged, and from that time the show never looked back. It enjoyed a long run of over two years and was an outstanding success, and in that success I, too, had my share, in the rôle of " Vanucci." It had originally been filled by Gilda Varesi, who was unfortunate enough to fall ill.

As I have already said, communications with Russia were extremely difficult and I had been many months without news of my husband.

Suddenly I received a letter from Trombetti, written from Rome, where he had been sent on an important mission by the Marchese Carlotti, the Italian Ambassador in Petrograd, whose right hand Trombetti had now become. My husband told me of his great joy in seeing his parents again, and how happy he was that he had been able to arrange to pass through London on his way back to his post in Russia. I was overjoyed, as otherwise we should not have been able to meet at that time.

He arrived one evening of September in 1916 whilst I was playing in *Romance*, so I could only meet him after the performance.

Nobody even suspected my marriage, hence many of the complications and difficulties for our meeting. But I will explain this later.

He remained with me for two days, after which followed more months of silence, as he returned to his post in Russia.

I still lived at St. Andrew's Mansions and I used to dine before going to the theatre at six-thirty, during which time it had become the habit of several leading members of the Italian colony, and a number of other friends, to drop in and eat the excellent fried potatoes which my maid Ersilia cooked in the way which Italians love and other mortals do not despise, and these were served with vermuth.

About this time I was rather indisposed in health and I imagined I was suffering from cancer of the stomach, which, unhappily, was rather prevalent then ; and the opinion was that it might be owing to the defective war-time food.

Notwithstanding my taking camomile tea and various other ingredients, I seemed to get worse and worse.

One morning I took my courage in both hands and, having made the appointment, I directed my footsteps to a stomach specialist in Harley Street, dreading in my heart that he would confirm my fears. On entering his consulting-room I hastily said to him : " I know I have cancer, so don't lie to me. I am already prepared for my end, and it is useless to pay for operations which are seldom of any ultimate use."

He seemed a bit bewildered as to how to answer me, but proceeded to examine me. The examination was brief, and with an amused smile he said : " You needn't make ready for your end yet, it is but a new beginning. You are to become a mother ! "

In spite of this, I continued my work at the theatre. On 6th June, 1917, I played my part in *Romance* as usual. After the matinée I went home for my dinner ; I suddenly felt so ill that I 'phoned Doris Keane that I dared not appear that evening.

At 9 a.m., on 7th June, 1917, my son Gianandrea was born.

CHAPTER VIII

FORETOLD FUTURE GLORIES!

ABOUT three months after my son's birth, Doris Keane was performing before a packed house at the Lyric Theatre, and at the end of the first act of *Romance* she fainted. As ill-luck would have it, her understudy was not in the theatre, and as Doris Keane was too ill to continue, it looked very much as though the performance would have to be abandoned. However, she sent me a message, and her manager, Louis Nethersole, begged me to carry on with her part and so avert the catastrophe.

Although I had not seen the rest of the play since the dress rehearsal, which was two years before, I agreed to do my best.

Louis Nethersole then went before the curtain, explained the situation to the audience, and asked for their indulgence and consideration. Meanwhile I was being hurriedly dressed for the second act, in which I carried " Adelina," the monkey, and a bunch of grapes for the monkey to bite, in case it should reveal a desire to bite my fingers. I was pushed on to the stage and the play continued. Then a very extraordinary thing happened to me : in my mind I saw all the details of the play as though I were watching it from the stalls. I began, also, to remember the story, although I naturally did not know the actual text. I had, therefore, to improvise.

Owen Nares and Cecil Humphreys, in their respective rôles of "Tom" and "Van Tuyll," succeeded with astonishing skill to pick up their cues, and we managed to carry the performance to a conclusion. Never shall I forget the enthusiasm, appreciation, and kindness of that night's audience.

At the end I was in such a state of nervous excitement that I walked home and patrolled Baker Street until two in the morning before I was able to settle down sufficiently to return to my home. I then collapsed into bed and slept the clock round.

Doris Keane subsequently made me a handsome present—a cheque for a hundred pounds—and I still possess the letter of thanks which Louis Nethersole wrote me, "for so gallantly saving the situation." Later, I was given the task of understudying the part of "Cavallini."

While *Romance* was running we had the additional excitement of the air raids. Sometimes we carried on with the performance, at other times all adjourned to the theatre cellars "for the duration."

My part in the play finished some time before the end of the final act, and I generally left the theatre about twenty minutes before the rest of my colleagues.

One evening there had been an alarm, but subsequently the "All Clear" was sounded, and we assumed there was now no danger. I walked to Piccadilly Circus, intending to take my usual bus 13 at Swan and Edgar's. No buses appearing, I then, for some curious reason, crossed over and continued to walk up the other side towards Oxford Circus, hoping to get a bus there. Not a soul was to be seen. Hardly had I crossed the road when it happened.

Curiously, I heard no sound, but felt the full force of the concussion. I leant for support on the shutters of the Goldsmith and Silversmith shop and looked across the street. What had been Piccadilly Circus had been flung into the air, the entire façade of the Swan and Edgar building had fallen, and not a window on that side of the road remained whole. Then, I am bound to admit, panic seized me, and I ran up the deserted Regent Street in a manner which would have earned me a place in the Olympic team of any country. Arriving at the tube station of Oxford Circus, I noticed that its entrance was filled with screaming, hysterical people, and so I continued on my way home, which I reached after what seemed an interminable age.

Far too often the Zeppelins paid us their unwelcome visits after we had settled ourselves in bed and had dropped off to sleep. At such times all occupants of my flat, i.e. my maid Ersilia, the baby André, and a pet mongrel dog, migrated to the basement, and with the other residents of the house stayed there until the danger had passed. Involuntarily, Ersilia caused a good deal of amusement and so did much to relieve the tension. While the bombs were dropping and the guns firing, she was on her knees praying fervently ; but when the sounds of battle had ceased she stood up and hurled fearful abuse at certain governments and heads of states—to fall on to her knees again at the first renewal of the firing and bomb-dropping. We were often too amused at her display of Southern temperament to feel any anxiety for ourselves.

In those days a very dear cousin lived with me, Isabel d'Inohan, her mother was Amelie Drummond and had married a Brazilian. During the reign of Pedro, Amelie had been Lady-in-Waiting at the Court in Rio de Janeiro.

As a means of obtaining some relief from the air raids and also in order to secure proper air and nourishment for the baby, when it arrived, I used to spend the week-ends at a charming little place, "Rushmeads," Horley, on the Surrey–Sussex borders, which Isabel and I had rented. We had there a poultry farm and a fine orchard, and for a long time were able to supply many of our friends with fresh eggs and fruit.

We put the farm in charge of Nurse Mulcaster, who had nursed my mother for many years before her death, and before that had been a maternity nurse. I had always promised her that if ever I had a child I should send for her, wherever she might be. In the meantime she had married a farmer and gone to live in Yorkshire. However, when she got my letter, down she came, and we installed her at Horley. She brought with her a beautiful Persian cat, which she adored, and would never go anywhere without! It was indeed a most charming and amazing sight to see this cat lying by the fire with dozens of little yellow fluffy chickens, just out of the incubator, nestling into its fur. Not only did the cat never touch them, but it regarded them with tender solicitude and purred with contentment.

We had a lovely orchard full of apple trees; one tree in particular was heavily laden with rosy apples, and we decided to get up early one morning and pick them, as we wanted to store some and make apply jelly of the others. So one morning at cock-crow we all arose, including another friend who was staying for the week-end, to begin our work. The air was sharp and fresh and we should much have preferred to remain in our warm beds. But the apples called us! When we approached the tree, without one word we all turned and gazed at each other! Not one apple left on the tree. . . . The mystery remains unsolved to this day. One can only conclude that somebody who knew the place had come during the night and . . . first come, first served!

We led a really rural life there, having our meals on the lawn during the summer, where our pet old duck, to whom I was much attached, used to waddle across the grass, having forsaken his pond for our company. The baby in the meantime was growing stronger, and Trombetti, on a short holiday, came down to see his son and help dig in the garden, which was a change for him from diplomacy.

It used to be quite a wrench every Monday afternoon when I had to come back to London for the theatre, and where my cooking at the flat was suffering deeply in the absence of Ersilia.

At last I found a good English nurse for the child, and Ersilia came back to her saucepans!

Suddenly, one morning, on coming into my room, Ersilia informed me that she felt very homesick and that she must leave at once to go and die in her own country. I tried to reason with her, but to no avail. Ersilia's home is up in the mountains in Italy, near Pistoia, not very far from Florence.

On the morning of Ersilia's departure, to my amazement, the butcher's boy of a shop in High Street, Marylebone, rang at the door of my flat and announced that he was downstairs with the motor van to fetch her luggage! Ersilia, hearing this conversation, bounced out of the kitchen, already dressed for her journey, and explained to me that as her mountain village lacked many comforts and necessities of life, she had bought many things and packed them into several trunks and hampers. Amongst the various articles she had bought were whalebones for corsets! We started for Victoria Station, Ersilia and I in a taxi, followed by the butcher's van with the name of the butcher painted in full on the sides. Every few minutes during the drive Ersilia leant out of the window to see if her treasures were safe, and once or twice when she nearly lost sight of the van, she waved excitedly to the butcher's boy. We drove up to the Continental side of the station, much to the amusement of the porters, one of whom was ordered by Ersilia to remove her baggage from the butcher's van. The registering alone of her "treasures" cost me £11 9s. 3d. !

Though I seldom see her now, we always write at Christmas and Easter. I shall never forget her great joy when three years ago she saw my son, whom she had not seen since he was quite a small boy.

She was a woman whose natural intelligence was above that of the ordinary peasant. When she had an evening out, and the Opera was on, she would go up to the gallery, and so musical was she, that next day she would be able to give a detailed criticism of each individual artist.

Before coming to me she had been, since the age of sixteen, with my friends, the Allievi. Signora Anna Allievi—Fanny's mother—was, and still is, very beautiful. Various well-know painters have painted her portrait, amongst others, Corcos. When he had finished her portrait, all the family assembled to pass their remarks and judge of the likeness. Everybody found it perfect and wonderful in every detail. Corcos said he would like to have Ersilia's opinion, as he had often noticed her extremely alert expression. She was therefore sent for, and she came up from the kitchen with a saucepan in her hand, which she was still stirring. ' She gave one look to Signora Allievi, one to the picture, and said : " *Naso storto !* " (Crooked nose), and walked out ! Corcos examined his work and remarked : " She's quite right," and rectified it.

Ersilia also had extraordinary knowledge about things that the ordinary people do not usually know. For instance, the origin of the name Campidoglio, which even to many Italians is not known, means oilfields (*campi*—fields, *olio*—oil). And to my surprise I heard Ersilia explaining this one day to my little boy, and telling him the historical legend that the Capitol was built on the most fertile olive groves as an omen that Rome would be one of the most prosperous cities of the world.

Towards the end of the war it was by no means uncommon on first-nights to send up to the stage little parcels of butter and eggs in place of the usual flowers. I personally saw a small half-pound packet of butter, tied up in gay ribbons, handed to Marie Tempest, and received apparently with genuine appreciation.

The death in November, 1918, of my cousin, Isobel d'Inohan, who was also my child's godmother, brought an end to the Horley days, for I was then acting in London and could not spare time to carry on our little home there by myself. Her death was a very deep grief to all who knew her, and she is still remembered with affection by all her schoolmates of the Convent of the Assumption in Kensington Square, where she was brought up.

The early post-war years were full of drama to myself, and particularly I remember that opening night of the *House of Peril*, which was in March, 1919. My baby had contracted double-pneumonia, and in the opinion of my medical advisor, Dr. Macdonald Brown, a fine old Scotsman, whose memory I shall always respect, it was unlikely that he would survive the night. But the kind old doctor insisted that I should go to the theatre as I could not be replaced, and promised to remain with the child until I returned. At the Queen's Theatre I ran into Owen Nares, who apparently noticed that I was worried and asked : "What was wrong?" I told him. After Act I, in which I had a long part, Owen Nares came up to me. He had in the meanwhile telephoned home to enquire what news there was. "Baby's all right," he said. "My car will take you home." This being his first venture as actor-manager, and as he must have had a thousand cares and tasks on that night, I appreciated to the full that act of kindly consideration. Having two boys of his own, to whom he is devoted, I think made him understand the anxiety I was going through.

During his convalescence Gianandrea contracted bronchitis !

At this point the reader will be interested to learn that through all this time my marriage had been kept a strict secret, not the least of the reasons being that as a diplomat on foreign service in time of war, and under Italian regulations, my husband had no right to marry without the consent of the Foreign Ministry, nor could he marry an actress who was still on the stage, not even if she were a royal princess.

When he came to London in 1917, that is shortly after the birth of our child, we naturally desired to make known our secret, and we began to discuss the best means of accomplishing this. The first person to be approached, and told in confidence of the marriage, was Signor Preziosi, Counsellor at the Italian Embassy in London, who was a great personal friend. Preziosi was horrified, and at once pointed out the grave seriousness of the step which we had taken. He explained that not only had Trombetti broken the rules by marrying without consent, he had also—a far more serious matter—been travelling on a diplomatic passport in which he was described as a "bachelor"! Continuing, Signor Preziosi said that Trombetti, now at the commencement of what promised to be a brilliant career, had by his rashness placed himself in a position which might bring instant dismissal from the Service. His advice was that the marriage should be further held a secret until Trombetti had firmly established himself in his career, and until sufficient time had passed for what he termed the "irregularities of the past" to be forgiven.

It was our friend's wish that, in order to confirm his views, we should consult Sir George Lewis, whom we went to see. The famous solicitor without hesitation supported Preziosi's viewpoint and advised us on no account to publish the marriage at that time.

After much heart-searching and many long discussions, my husband and I finally decided to adopt the course which, we had been advised, was the best in the circumstances.

Trombetti was terribly disappointed and, indeed, shocked by this turn which he had certainly not expected. He resolved to throw every ounce of his energies and every minute of his time into his work and do his utmost to advance as quickly as possible to a position in which he would have nothing more to fear.

He was appointed private secretary to Signor Nitti, and in that capacity was present at all the Paris Peace Conferences. The letters which I received from him during that time were among the most interesting that I have ever read, and full of love for his little boy, and anxiety for me.

Later he became private secretary to Count Sforza.

One day, in October, 1920—another three years had passed—I received a letter from Rome in which Trombetti acquainted me with the splendid news that he had been appointed Minister to one of the Latin-American States. He asked me to come at once to Rome so that we could publish the marriage. I replied that I would be leaving London in about ten days.

Before leaving, I went to see Signor Preziosi at the Embassy, told him the news, and said also that I was breaking my journey in Paris to stay with Countess Regina de Oliveira, sister of the Brazilian Ambassador. Preziosi was delighted, and knowing the Oliveiras well, gave me a number of messages to carry to my friend. I arrived in Paris; Regina fetched me at the station and we went home to her flat.

At about six o'clock in the evening, while I was talking to her, the telephone rang. After a brief conversation, Regina turned to me, and from her manner and embarrassed look I could tell that she had heard news of a serious nature.

" You must return to London at once," she said to me.

" But I've just come from there," I replied. " I'm on my way to Rome, as you know."

Then she told me that Signor Preziosi had 'phoned to say that information had just been received from Rome that Trombetti had been the victim of a heart attack, and had collapsed on his own doorstep. He died almost immediately.

There was nothing for me to do but to return to London, and on my arrival I at once went to see the Italian Ambassador and his wife, the Marchese and Marchesa Imperiali.

Marchese Imperiali was appalled when I informed him of my marriage, and by the news of its tragic termination. He stated emphatically that the marriage must be announced without delay and that a telegram must be sent to my godmother, Queen Margherita. The message was despatched.

"Come to Rome at once," Her Majesty wired back.

On reaching Rome I announced my arrival to Queen Margherita, who sent a message that she wished to see me at once. My audience with Her Majesty lasted three hours. The news of my secret marriage had been a great shock to the Queen, who had always taken the kindliest interest in my affairs, and who, very naturally, had expected me, her godchild, to consult her before taking a step of so serious a nature.

Her Majesty, with great affection, but much gravity, spoke to me of the heavy responsibility I had assumed in keeping my marriage secret, not only for the consequences that might have fallen on me, but also on the child.

Gianandrea had from birth been a delicate child, and his care, especially in view of my weak financial position, became a problem of considerable magnitude. My husband's parents, who have always shown the greatest affection for, and interest in the progress of, their grandson, were more than willing to support me and my son in Rome, but in view of the fact that they were not millionaires, and that I was earning very good money here, I did not wish to be a burden to my people.

Queen Margherita discussed this problem with me at great length, and in the end not only gave her consent, but advised me to continue my career on the stage, in which profession I had already achieved some success. For numerous reasons there could be no question of my joining the stage in Rome where, in any case, the status of an actor was an exceedingly poor one. The only course open to me was to return to England and, as Queen Margherita advised, bring up my son with every care.

My late husband's parents, Signor and Signora Trombetti, own and occupy a house near the Teatro Argentina. At the time of which I am writing it was not of very considerable value. Now, by a strange stroke of fortune, it has suddenly become a very valuable property. That great architect, the Duce, has recently put into force a great programme of building in this part of Rome, and in the course of pulling down a number of old houses, another forum

M

has been discovered in the close neighbourhood of the Trombettis' house. Its value has increased enormously. My "in-laws" naturally wanted to see their only grandson as soon as possible, but as the child was so delicate we decided that his grandmother should come over to London to see the little fellow.

In England once more, I occupied myself for some time in translating Italian plays for C. B. Fernald. It was during that time that my cousin, Lady Victoria Manners, herself a landscape painter of great talent, commissioned me to translate the manuscript diary of Angelica Kauffmann, which is kept in the library of the Royal Academy at Burlington House. This interesting document, of course, was not let out, and I had to go to Burlington House daily and work there. The diary was written in such small handwriting that I could only read it with the aid of a magnifying glass.

About this time I met at a very smart tea-party an extraordinary little man with an amazing personality. My hostess introduced me to him, hoping he might be able to put me in touch with some theatrical managers. He replied that he knew nobody connected with the stage, that his friends were only important City and business men, but that if he could in any way advise me about my finances, he would be delighted to do so. A few days later he rang me up and told me that he knew of a wonderful investment giving 12 per cent, but that he could not name it over the 'phone. As my income then was already somewhat diminished, I jumped at this chance and asked him to come at once to see me.

He was a curious-looking little man, far from

distinguished, bald, clean-shaven, and had extraordinary green eyes.

On arriving at the house he showed me a lot of photographs of huge factory buildings which, he said, were in the North of England, and whose shares would yield this big dividend. He showed me also heaps of documents concerning this enterprise and a letter from my friend at whose house I had met him, which proved to me that she had already invested £20,000 in his concern. Most stupidly I did not consult my lawyer, but I sold out some of my securities and handed over some thousands of pounds to this man. He informed me that he was taking offices in the Strand, and that he would like me very much to see them. So, accordingly, a friend and I went over there one day. We were struck by the million dollar atmosphere, and I felt more than reassured about my money. There were soft pile carpets under our feet and tall commissionaires with ultra smart uniforms. The offices themselves were most luxurious, and typists and secretaries were busily employed. On one occasion, when he asked me to go and see him on a matter of extreme importance concerning my investment, I was shown into his own private office, where he sat practically hidden behind a huge desk, and to my amazement, hanging on the wall at the back of him, was a big modern oil painting of Our Lord as a child. The little man, whom we shall now call " Mr. A," saw me regarding the picture with surprise, and addressed me as follows : " For this I have sent for you, Mary Magdalen, to reveal to you your real identity, as I shall reveal mine to you. The picture you are gazing at is myself as a child. My other partner in this firm is St. Peter." I was more than taken aback, and somewhat puzzled as to the outcome of this and wondered if my money was quite safe under the circumstances ! He added that if ever I were ill I was to let him know, as St. Luke was also in the company, under the disguise of a real physician. He went on to say that very soon I should be recognised as a great power when, on the opening of Joanna Southcott's box in Trafalgar Square (which was to happen shortly), I should be sitting there with the bishops ; and at the very moment that the box would open, a great stream of light would fall on me, after which the bishops and people would render homage to me. At this prospect of my future glory I felt most elated !

The odd thing is that although fundamentally I did not believe it, all this did not seem to me so extraordinary as it does to the reader. In looking back there is no doubt that the man possessed the gift and, to me, dangerous weapon of hypnotism.

On leaving, after this tirade, Mr. A accompanied me through the passage and led me into another room where sat the lesser lights, St. Peter and St. Luke. It seemed to my carnal mind that St. Luke was slightly the worse for drink !

I must confess that after I left, I had my doubts about Mr. A. But as my 12 per cent came in regularly and all the appearances of the business were solid, I and other friends who had equally placed money in his hands, came to the conclusion that, although a very clever business man, he had a maggot in his brain on that subject which, after all, did not affect us materially.

All went well for over two years, then suddenly,

when my dividends were due, they failed to appear. I waited a week, then telephoned, but could get no answer, so I took a 13 bus (13 for luck !) and rushed down to the Strand. On reaching the " Temple " (as he used to call his offices), I found it deserted ; doors shut, commissionaires gone ; the company of saints had disappeared ! With horror I rushed off to my lawyer, but, alas ! nothing could be done. They tried to discover Mr. A's whereabouts, but it was impossible to trace him. We found out that the photos he had shown us were of real existing factories, but not his ! He had made several victims ; the only one who never knew her misfortune and had died in the meantime undeceived, was the friend at whose house I had met him.

I felt my financial loss all the more as I had my child to bring up and look after. He was at this time about four years old, a bright, attractive little fellow with fair hair and grey-blue eyes, and resembling very much my mother.

He was at the age when children begin asking the continual " Why ? " that is generally so difficult to answer.

One day whilst sitting in the drawing-room with the cat, dog, and baby, I noticed him looking very intently at the animals in question. He scrambled on to my knee, and with a very grave expression he said : " Mummy ! Pussy four legs, doggie four legs, Baby only two. Why ? " I tried to explain to him that animals and human beings are different, we being superior ; but I could quite see that he thought he had been done out of two legs !

It was a great consolation in my loneliness, to give my little boy his first religious teachings, and I tried to depict the various episodes of Our Lord's life as vividly as possible. The results were at times rather disconcerting ! I was still in bed one morning and the child was playing about on the floor in my room when I saw him take one of my boots, put it into my wardrobe with a very determined face, close the door, and then seize an old black doll he had, and beat it mercilessly. He was red in the face, and his eyes flashed. I stopped him, and asked what was the matter. He then told me that the black doll was the wicked man who had killed Jesus Christ, and that he (Andrea) had buried Our Lord in the sepulchre, which was the wardrobe. I was speechless !

My son is really called Gianandrea, which is the amalgamation of Giovanni and Andrea (John and Andrew), two of the most ancient of our Vitelleschi family names ; it is usual in Italy to link thus two together. Various of my friends are called Gianluca (John-Luke), Giancarlo (John-Charles), and so forth.

It is interesting to note that every Italian, whether man or woman, is baptised " Maria " in honour of the Blessed Virgin, as well as their other names.

My great ambition was that my son should, like myself, speak various languages, so I had a French nurse for him who started calling him André, and by force of habit we all followed suit. I spoke Italian to him, and I taught him the days of the week in the same way as my father taught me, and as he himself had been taught by his parents. It was a very quaint way, and appeals to a child's imagination. It is as follows :

Lunedi ando da *Martedi*
perch' andasse da *Mercoledi*
per sapere da *Giovedi*
se *Venerdi* aveva inteso
da *Sabato* che *Domenica* era festa !

This is the translation :

Monday went to *Tuesday*
asking it to go to *Wednesday*
to find out from *Thursday*
whether *Friday* had heard from
Saturday that *Sunday* was a feast day !

A very strange thing happened to me at this time ;
but to make the reader realise the curious coincidence
which led up to a rather extraordinary theory, on
the part of several who know me, I must return for
a brief moment to my childhood. My parents and
I used to often stay for a few days in Florence, on
our return to Rome from London and Paris. We
had many friends and relations there as, in the past,
a Nobili of Florentine origin married a Vitelleschi,
and to this day every Vitelleschi bears the name
Nobili. Much as I loved staying in different places,
and seeing fresh faces, the one town in the world
I loathed was Florence. As soon as we arrived there,
I was seized with the most terrible depression and
terror. I appreciated and valued the beauty of all
the things around me, but nothing could shake
off my inexplicable fear. At night I could not sleep,
and often my nurse sat beside me an hour or so,
trying to calm me. She endeavoured in vain to
discover the origin of my fear ; but I could not
explain, as I did not know myself. By the time we

left Florence I was really ill, so much so, that finally my parents decided that when next they went there, they would not take me with them. Another strange factor in this story is that I have always had a horror of daggers, and an intense dislike of ever going a sea voyage.

As everyone will remember, during and after the war, a great wave of Spiritualism swept through England, for so many had lost those they loved; it was an outcome of intense desire to be in contact with those who meant so much to them. The occult has always fascinated me, and I became a sincere believer, though I quite realised that notwithstanding its comforts, some dangers might attend it. With a great sense of diffidence and expectancy I went to my first séance. The medium was very well known, and had a great many followers. It was a full quarter of an hour before she went into a trance and then to my amazement she said : " Piero." I replied that I knew nobody of that name. She then poured forth good Italian, and as I knew for a fact she knew no languages whatsoever, it surprised me all the more. This is exactly what she said : " You are Piero. Piero de Medici. Your portrait is in Florence —Uffizi Gallery—painted by Botticelli—you were drowned at the age of thirty-two. Try to change your character—don't make the same mistakes as in the past." I left feeling somewhat disconcerted, and for the time I could not even recall to my mind the picture she had mentioned. A few weeks later I went to tea with a fellow-actor, and there I met a friend of his, a very cultivated man. On being introduced to the latter, I noticed that he looked at me very intently. After a few minutes' conversation he said to me : " Excuse me staring at you so, but you are the very image of Botticelli's portrait of Piero de Medici. Do you by any chance believe in reincarnation ? Personally, I do." I then told him all that had occurred when I went to the medium, and also the strange feelings I had as a child when visiting Florence. They now seemed to have a *raison d'être* for me. He advised me to buy a print of the picture and to look up the life of Piero as he was sure it would interest me. The next day I went off to the Medici Galleries in Grafton Street. As I entered, an elderly woman was arranging some pictures on a table. I asked her for a cheap copy of Botticelli's Piero de Medici, which she immediately said she had, and went to fetch from the other side of the shop. As she came towards me with it in her hands, she exclaimed : " Why, you are exactly like the picture, Madam. It gives me quite a turn." That evening I read up Piero's life, and I was deeply interested to see that some of the traits of his character were not unlike my own ; for instance, the things he desired so much in life never seemed to come to him ; he was of a kind and generous disposition, but, unfortunately, too easily influenced by people who gave him advice. He was most artistic, and preferred that sort of life to politics. After being exiled from Florence he was drowned at the age of thirty-two, when the ship he was in, capsized. His nickname was Piero the Unfortunate.

Of course, many people are not believers in reincarnation, neither are they believers in communications between the so-called dead and the living.

I must say that in these days when science and

communications in every way are so advanced, nothing seems impossible to me. We must pause for a moment and realise that if a hundred years ago somebody had suddenly come into a room with a box, and placed it on the floor, turned a knob, and by thus doing had filled the room with a concert from Vienna or a song from the Opera in Paris or even a speech from New York, he would have been accused of black magic.

So how do we know that in a hundred years hence we shall not be able to communicate freely with those who have passed into the Great Beyond.

CHAPTER IX

QUEEN MARGHERITA PASSES

IN April, 1923, I played in *The Outsider*. It was a play by Dorothy Brandon about osteopathy, a branch of surgery which at that time was causing a good deal of public commotion. There was much hostility between the recognised medical societies and the bone-setters, the "quacks," who in the majority of cases were unqualified practitioners. Thus the play possessed a strong topical interest.

Leon M. Lion, the producer, had offered me the part of "Madame Klost," that of a poor woman suffering from hip disease, who walked with a limp. She was cured by the osteopath. Mr. Lion was a wonder producer and it was he who taught me to limp in so convincing a manner that I myself almost imagined that I had been lame for life. He has an inimitable way of imparting to his actors and actresses just the actions and atmosphere which he desires of them. He has, too, a remarkable enthusiasm that is infectious. He was an inspiration to every member of the cast.

We had for this play a "star" cast, including Isobel Elsom, Leslie Faber, who was outstanding in the part of the quack, Dawson Milward and Lyall Swete.

We were opening for a week at Folkestone to give the play a "try-out" before taking it to London.

On 26th April, that is four days before the opening
night, I became very ill with bronchitis and I had a
high temperature. Dr. Macdonald Brown stated
that there was the danger of complications, especially
of pneumonia, and he strictly forbade me to attend
the last rehearsals. I therefore telephoned Leon
M. Lion, who at once replied that it was imperative
that I should be at the final rehearsal, as they could
not carry on without me.

André's nurse then happened to mention that she
had heard that an old-fashioned and very efficacious
safeguard to prevent bronchitis was a brown paper
waistcoat. I decided to give it a trial.

With my chest and back swathed in layers of
brown paper, which rustled horribly with every
step I took, I set out for Folkestone and went to the
final night rehearsal—with a temperature of 103!

When my Folkestone landlady came to enquire
about my meals I asked, to her visible and expressed
astonishment, for large supplies of oranges, Italian
vermuth and hot water, out of which I concocted a
beverage. I lived on that, and nothing else, for three
days. At any other time, if anyone had suggested
mixing me this "cocktail," I would have been
horrified, but during those days something within
me seemed to cry out for it.

The First Night came, the piece was enthusiastically received, and the audience gave me a great
ovation. After three days, instead of finding myself
in hospital, I made the glad discovery that I was
cured. My temperature was normal, and my voice
had lost its huskiness, a circumstance which, I soon
found, pleased me better than my producer.

"What's happened to the wheeze?—it was

admirable," said Mr. Lion on the fourth night. I explained that it had been due to the bronchitis. Mr. Lion, without wishing me any harm, was sorry that I was not going to have bronchitis for the rest of the " run."

Three weeks later we transferred to the St. James's in London, where *The Outsider* enjoyed a gratifying success.

As soon as I had an opportunity, I asked Dr. Macdonald Brown for an explanation of my cure. I told him of the oranges and vermuth. He thought that there might be something in the instinct that had prompted that craving, and that the oranges and vermuth (which is manufactured from white wine, gentian, oranges, angelica, etc.) in all probability provided precisely the ingredients containing the medicinal properties which cured me. He added that he was a firm believer in people's individual instincts when they were ill, if they craved for any particular food or drink ; as his experience had shown him that very often Nature knew better than the doctor what was good for the patient.

It was during the run of *The Outsider* in London that a very amusing thing happened to me. One wet night, when it was blowing a gale, I was waiting for my bus after the theatre, at Piccadilly Circus. I had on my mackintosh, goloshes, an old beret, and I was literally hanging on to my umbrella. Walking up and down, also waiting for a bus, I imagined, was another lady ; and I was thinking how wet her fur coat was getting. Suddenly she came up to me, pushed my arm, and said : " Here you ; get off my beat ! " Although somewhat taken aback, my sense of humour rose to the occasion, as nobody could have looked less like one of the ladies she took me for, as I in the get-up I have described. " I am on nobody's beat ; I am only waiting for my bus and praying to God that it will come soon," was my reply. With that I hopped onto my bus which at that moment appeared.

A few days after, as I was walking down Baker Street, I came across one of the old gardeners whom I had employed at Horley. Seeing him reminded me of a really funny thing that happened just before I left " Rushmeads."

This man was a little wizened creature with a mangy moustache ; nevertheless at a carnival that was held near Horley, he appeared in the procession as a Cavalier ! He was attired in velvet doublet and hose, much too big for him, high boots, a red velvet cloak, and a huge Cavalier's hat with feathers. He had a long sword which flapped against the flanks of the huge white cart-horse he sat on ! (I cannot say he rode !) So grotesque did he appear that as he passed, shrieks of laughter rang forth from the spectators. But he heeded them not ; such was his conceit that he imagined himself the central figure in the procession. He prinked and he perked, and finally, forgetting that his wig was fixed to his hat, he swept the latter off with a great flourish, revealing a little bald head ! The amusement of the crowd knew no bounds, and the little man took it for admiration !

Meanwhile, *Romance* had been translated into French by Robert de Flers and Francis de Croisset. Doris Keane, having made enquiries in Paris, found that there was no Italian actress who could fill my old rôle of " Vannucci," and she therefore insisted that I should again take this part in the French version.

I arrived in Paris on 1st December and met my new comrades, with whom I was to appear at the Théâtre Athenee. In the French cast were, among others, Lucien Rozenberg, the Director of the theatre, in the rôle of " Van Tuyll," Madeleine Soria, his wife, who was to play " Cavallini," and Paul Bernard, " Tom." I was given a most kindly reception by my new French friends, who did everything in their power to make my stay among them a pleasant one.

We spent four weeks in rehearsing—four weeks of hard work, during which the production studied the minutest details with a thoroughness that I have never experienced elsewhere. But if the work was harder, and the production more thorough than at the English rehearsals, it was made infinitely pleasant by the natural friendship shown by everyone concerned and by the admirable *camaraderie* which existed between all the members of the company. I soon discovered there is a genuine *esprit de corps* which makes the work of everyone not only more agreeable but more efficient. The highest-paid actor greets his lowest-paid *confrère* with the same cordiality and naturalness that he shows towards the more successful members of the profession. Among the actors there is almost a family spirit.

One small incident impressed on me the importance which French producers attach to what some would be inclined to dismiss as negligible details. In the play there is a very minor part of the " Footman." He appears on the scene carrying a tray on which are two decanters, one with white wine and the other red. He sets down the tray, and without saying a single word, leaves the stage. A very simple matter, most people would say, which anyone could learn to do successfully in a few minutes. At the first rehearsal the footman came on, put down the tray, and went off. Immediately Lucien Rozenberg called him back and in the kindliest manner broke the news to him that his performance was " rotten."

" Have you never watched a really first-class waiter ? " asked Rozenberg.

The young actor modestly explained that he could not afford to visit the best restaurants and hotels, and so was not familiar with the ways of " first-class " servants. " All right," said Rozenberg, " we'll soon remedy that." He 'phoned to the " Café de Paris " and asked them if they would send one of their waiters to give a demonstration. The waiter spent two hours a day for two days before Lucien Rozenberg pronounced himself satisfied with the performance of his " footman."

We opened at the Théâtre Athenee on Christmas Eve. I was suffering from an acute attack of stage fright. It was my first appearance before a hyper-critical Parisian audience, and I wondered anxiously whether I should survive the test. However, as soon as I found myself on the stage my fright was forgotten, I put everything into my part—and received one of the heartiest receptions that has ever been accorded me. The play was an instant success with the Paris theatre-going public and its popularity was well sustained until May, 1924, when Madeleine Soria had the misfortune to suffer a nervous break-down. It was then taken off.

There was great rejoicing behind the stage on the First Night. Robert de Flers, de Croisset, and several others came to my dressing-room, and there were many embraces and congratulations. After the performance we were all invited to a supper party, which was one of the happiest and merriest occasions that I have ever attended.

On many other nights I went with Lucien Rozenberg, or one of the other leading actors—generally there was a little party of us—to the Café de la Madeleine on the Boulevard of that name, where over a glass of wine we sat and talked. We discussed matters of topical interest, art, persons, politics to a certain extent, and many other subjects. They were happy little occasions, which, to me, were like a mental tonic.

It was during this stay in Paris that I met a very interesting personality in Monsieur Corpechot, who was then editor of *Le Gaulois*, a literary paper which has since amalgamated with another journal. M. Corpechot had seen me in *Romance* and as a result of the favourable impression which he had gained wished to interview me.

He was a man of exceptional culture and a most capable conversationalist, and so before long we were talking of the stage and many other subjects in which both of us were interested. During our conversation he learnt that Stella Rho was Stella Vitelleschi, the daughter of his great friend. He told me how much he had admired my father, his political opinions and his wonderful outlook and what interesting talks they had had together whilst dining sometimes at the famous restaurant " Foyot."

They had often discussed, during his stays in

N

Paris, their pet theme of Franco-Italian friendship. My father had always held—and his view was wholeheartedly endorsed by M. Corpechot—that two countries that had so much in common as Italy and France, and whose interests so often ran parallel to each other, should stand side by side. The Marchese's wish was to see an Anglo-French-Italian *bloc* for the preservation of European peace.

Gianandrea, or André, as his French nurse called him, was now six years old, and I was anxious for him to learn early to be independent, especially as he had no father. Accordingly, whilst I was playing in *Romance* in Paris, I sent instructions to his nurse, Germaine, to send him over to me by himself for Christmas, and for her to come by the next train. In those days I used to travel a lot to and fro between Paris and London, so I knew very well all the officials along the line and on the boat; I wrote to several of them, telling them of my plan and asking them to keep an eye on the child and hand him from one to the other. Germaine put him into the train and under the charge of the guard at Victoria Station, and I was to fetch him at the Gare du Nord in Paris. I confess I felt a little nervous at the result of my experiment, and I set forth very early to meet the train. Punctual to the minute the train steamed into the station, and as usual the crowd pouring out of the carriages was great. Through the hustle and bustle of porters, passengers, and suit-cases, I stood on tip-toe looking for the small figure of my son. At last I saw a small, fat form in a sailor cap and coat, stolidly walking down the platform towards me. As he approached, I saw something peculiar hanging round his neck;

I could not make out what it was until I got quite close; and then I saw it was a wide red ribbon, and from it hung his passport, flapping on his chest as he walked. On my asking if he had been frightened travelling alone, he looked up at me with a very serious little face and said: "No; now I am grown up enough to look after you."

After leaving Paris and before returning to London I accepted the invitation of an old friend to visit the Hague. Lucia Slade was the daughter of General Slade, and I had known her when her father was British Military Attaché in Rome, when we were both children.

General and Mrs. Slade, who afterwards became Sir John and Lady Slade, were amongst my parents' greatest friends in Rome, and they lived in a charming house in Piazza Trinità dei Monti, near the Villa Medici, close to one of the entrances to the Pincio. Lady Slade was a Miss Wood, and it was her family who owned the lovely house at Shepperton which has now been turned into film studios. It was there that Lady Slade had spent her childhood, and I know it was a great grief to her when it was sold. Although Lucia was a few years older than I was, which as children makes a great difference, I often used to go out with her and her governess for walks in the Pincio. I remember so well envying the hard straw hat with the coloured riband band she wore, which was then the fashion for grown-ups.

At the time about which I am now writing, she was married to Sir Charles Marling, who at this time held the post of British Minister at the Dutch Court.

The Minister and his wife occupied a charming old house at the Hague, whose one disadvantage was the absence of sufficient bathrooms. For the guest-rooms on the first floor there was only one bathroom, and so it frequently happened that guests passing to and fro, met in the corridor leading to it.

The Grand-Duchess Marie, a sister of the Grand-Duke Dmitri of Russia, was also a guest at the British Legation during one of my visits there. She is a charming personality, full of vivacity, and has a great sense of humour. Her Imperial Highness and I used to meet in Lucia's boudoir every evening at six o'clock for an hour before dressing for dinner, and the three of us vied with each other in telling the most amusing anecdotes. I well remember how they laughed when I told them the following : In a provincial town in Italy, a man who held a very important position and who was a friend of a relation of mine died. As everybody knows, in Italy the body is always watched : therefore, after the deceased was laid out on his bed and covered with flowers, the family placed to watch him throughout the night, a man who had helped to nurse him. Early next day the family, attired in deep mourning, entered the room, and to their horror saw, sleeping on the bed by the side of their beloved parent, the watcher ! To make room for himself he had pushed some of the wreaths aside, and others were resting on his chest ! On being violently awakened by the indignant family he humbly apologised, but gave as an excuse for his unpardonable conduct that he had done so much watching lately that he could not keep awake !

Another still more amusing story I told them was the following : I was once the guest of a well-known hostess, and a mutual friend of ours was there at the same time. She used to go out to dances and entertainments nearly every night and was not back till four or five in the morning. This became rather remarked upon, so my hostess considered it her friendly duty to warn her she was being talked about, and that people might say she was having an affair with somebody. "What does it matter," replied our friend, " a lover at night is like an apple a day, it keeps the doctor away ! "

Friendly as we all were, naturally, the Grand-Duchess had to be accorded the etiquette which is due to royalty.

One morning, as I was going to take my bath, I met her in the passage. I was carrying on my arm a big bath-towel, on the end of which was a long fringe. I said : " *Bonjour*, Altesse," and curtsied. As I did so, my foot caught in the fringe of the towel and I fell on the floor. Her Imperial Highness tried to prevent me falling, and in doing so nearly fell herself.

I was taken by my hosts to many of the Dutch beauty spots and to several of those delightful country houses which are so characteristic of Holland. And in the evenings, after dinner, we generally went to the Restaurant Royal to listen and dance to one of the finest *cigany* bands that I have ever heard—and we had heard many in Rome. The restaurant was the favourite rendezvous of the foreign diplomats and the younger members of the Dutch aristocracy, and their enthusiasm, kept at high pitch by the fiery chords of the gipsy band, had to be seen to be realised.

Dear Lucia Marling died a few years later in a terrible motor accident near Dieppe.

After the all-too-brief holiday I returned to work, and in April, 1925, played in the first revival of *Romance* in Paris. Following a successful run, we opened for a week in Lyon, where the change of air seemed to exercise a beneficial effect on the whole company. Our appetite was prodigious ; there seemed hardly enough food in that great city to satisfy it.

We played there at the Théâtre des Celestins, which is one of the best known throughout France ; a very excellent restaurant of the same name stands on the opposite side of the big square facing the theatre, and gave us special terms for meals that made us realise what the food of the Gods on the Parnassus must have been like! We were a most cheerful, happy company ; in that revival it was Roger Gaillard who played the part of " Tom," and the part of " Suzette," the eighteen-year-old granddaughter in the prologue and epilogue, was then played by a lovely and charming, fair-haired, blue-eyed girl of seventeen. It was the first time she had left her home, and her mother anxiously asked Rozenberg whether there was anybody in the company who could take charge of her. Before we left Paris he introduced me to the mother, saying : " Here is Stella Rho, and I know that she will take as much care of your daughter as you would." So during this week's tour, wherever Stella went the little girl went, too. She is now a famous French film star, Dolly Davies. Spite her English name and parentage, she had lived since her birth in France and seemed entirely French.

Another fact that will interest those who saw *Romance* during the war in London is that the now famous young " premier " in Paris, Fernand Gravey, is the son of the unforgettable Mertens who played the old *maître d'hôtel* with us here, and who, unhappily, died during the run of the play.

Before falling ill, Mertens asked me whether I would be the godmother at the Confirmation of his little son Fernand. It is the custom in the Roman Catholic Church for every child to have a godmother at his or her Confirmation. I accepted with pleasure.

When I went to Paris a few years later to play in *Romance*, I found, to my surprise and delight, that the part of the grandson, " Harry," was going to be played by my own godson, Fernand.

I enjoyed my week in Lyon from every point of view ; in the first place, when touring in France with a Paris management, it is the manager who makes all the arrangements for the accommodation of the company, so one has not the trouble of looking for rooms. Secondly, added to the salary, one is given a settled daily sum called *indemnité de séjour* to compensate the extra expense one is forcibly put to, when living away from home.

Lyon itself was of great interest to me personally, as there are so many Roman remains there. When I went up the funiculaire to Notre Dame de Fourvière, which is well known for its riches and the wonderful view one gets from its summit, I wondered how many of my own countrymen had, in the past, trod that same way.

The name of Notre Dame de Fourvière, which as well as a beauty site is also the goal of thousands of pilgrims every year, derives its origin from Forum Vetus. On this spot stood a Roman forum, over which in the ninth century was built a small chapel, the original Notre Dame de Fourvière. This lovely town is divided by the two well-known rivers, the Rhône and the Saône, over which twenty-four wide bridges are built.

On seeing this populated, commercial town full of tramways, private cars, people busily running to and fro, I tried to picture what Lyon looked like when Nero helped to rebuild it after it had been destroyed by fire in A.D. 59. It seemed a queer contrast to me that he should have helped to rebuild Lyon and yet he himself sat and watched his own Rome burn from a tower still existing in Via Nazionale, whilst playing the violin. In my spare hours I made a special point of going to see some of the old baths and the relics of the Roman theatre. All these memories of the various emperors, amongst which Trajan and Adrian really made me feel as if I had suddenly been transported back to Rome.

At the end of our week we travelled back to Paris after the night performance. Rozenberg and his wife, Madeleine Soria, got into their sleeper, taking with them " Adelina " the little monkey in the play. A whole second-class coach was reserved for our company. As soon as we entered the train my " adopted daughter " Dolly installed herself comfortably with her head on my lap and slept serenely all night. I was, needless to say, not so comfortable ! When we arrived the following morning in Paris at the Gare de Lyon we all met upon the platform, before separating to go to our various homes. As Rozenberg and Soria descended from their sleeping car, we noticed that she was crying bitterly and that Rozenberg looked upset. In her arms she carried the dead body of poor " Adelina."

We then learnt that to keep the little creature warm, which is so necessary for monkeys, Soria had enveloped it completely in her big fur coat. Evidently in some way the monkey had got entangled in the inside of the coat, thus completely closing out any air, and suffocation was the cause of its death. Being asleep, neither Monsieur nor Madame Rozenberg had noticed its cries or its struggles. The next monkey that Soria got for the following performance of *Romance* was also a delightful little creature, and very amusing. To avoid the dangers of consumption, which they are so liable to contract, Soria had made him various little coloured flannel pneumonia jackets with a big " A " embroidered on the front. This new little " Adelina " was extremely particular about the colour of his coats ; he had an intense dislike to green. Whenever this green coat appeared upon the scenes, the anger of this little monkey was so great and he chattered so furiously that the coat had to be put away again.

I remained in Paris for some while longer and joined Edward Stirling's Repertory Company of English Players, in which the famous Ben Greet was a prominent personality.

They had rented the small Théâtre Albert I in rue des Rochers, and we used to give there the latest London successes.

After a happy association with that company I accepted an offer from the Pitoeffs to act at the Théâtre des Arts in one of Pirandello's plays.

Its French title was *Comme ci et comme ça.*

From the first rehearsal Georges Pitoeff swore us all to secrecy as to one of its most important items, which if it leaked out in any possible way before

the production, would be detrimental to the unexpected surprise of the play; hence destroying
a main factor of its first-night success.

After three weeks' rehearsal the night arrived.
The theatre was packed to capacity, not a seat was
vacant. Arrayed in a beautiful white evening dress
with my hair wonderfully arranged, I sat in one of
the stage boxes, at the back of which was one of
my fellow-actors. Before the curtain went up, and
during the first interval we talked and laughed
together as though we were ordinary theatregoers.
The three knocks gave the signal for the lights to go
out, and the curtain went up for the second act.
The scene portrayed an exact replica of the " foyer "
of the Théâtre des Arts. Many artists, who had
not appeared until then, walked about the stage
foyer, talking to each other and eagerly discussing
the first act of our play as though they were members
of the public. Suddenly, to the amazement of the
real audience, I jumped up, leant out of my box
and in very excited tones addressed the people on
the stage in the following words : " I consider it an
absolute outrage that one's private life should be
exposed by authors to the public. I shall sue for
damages." My companion in the box tried to calm
me, but of no avail, I continued expostulating.
The people on the stage, dismayed at this attack on
them and horrified at the disturbance I was creating,
crowded to the footlights towards my box and tried
in vain to explain to me that neither they, nor the
author, knew anything about me or my private life.
By this time the *real* public was in a state of ferment.
From all parts of the house there were cries of:
" Turn her out. . . . Stop her. . . . Shame. . . .

Turn on the lights. . . . Fetch the police. . . ." and such-like exclamations. In the midst of this turmoil a commissionaire was seen to enter my box, catch firmly hold of my arm and lead me away. My companion followed me. A sigh of relief passed through the audience and all eyes were again directed towards the stage with increased interest, as they had begun to wonder whether, perhaps, there was some truth in what I had said.

The actors in the meantime were also discussing who this mad woman was, when angry voices were heard in the wings, and, to the renewed indignation of the public, I rushed on to the stage like a fury, insulting all those who were on it.

It was only then that it began to dawn upon the public that it was the second act of the play. When the curtain came down there was an uproar of applause and *Comme ci comme ça* was a great success.

On that night I met the author for the first time. Much to my surprise I found him to be a small, modest man with a quiet, unassuming air. He had attended none of the rehearsals, having been perfectly content to rely on the production to give his play efficient and conscientious treatment.

His confidence was justified.

As the reader will remember, Pirandello died only a few months ago.

One of my great friends in Paris is Gabrielle Dorziat, the famous actress, and a most charming personality. A few years ago she married Comte Michel de Zogheb, who is so well known for his polo. He keeps several ponies in England for when he comes over to play here.

I originally met Dorziat at the Princess of Monaco's luncheon parties at Claridge's here in London, and we soon became great friends, and she gave me many useful hints regarding the art of acting.

All those who saw Bernstein's *Espoir* are unanimous in saying her rendering of the part was amongst the most beautiful pieces of acting ever seen.

I was still in Paris in January, 1926, and planning to spend a holiday at Rapallo, when I was saddened by the news of the death of Queen Margherita, who I knew had been ill for a long time with bronchitis. Two days before I was due to leave for Rapallo, Conte Nardini, who was Italian Consul in Paris and a very old friend of the family, rang up very early in the morning to tell me that the news had been officially received. He had been instructed to tell me, as the Queen's godchild, to go into mourning for a period of six months.

Queen Margherita had died at Bordighera, and her body was to be taken to Rome for interment in the Pantheon, where the remains of Victor Emmanuel II, and of her husband, King Umberto, also lay. On arriving at Rapallo I was informed by the local authorities of the time when the Royal funeral *cortège* would halt at the station on its journey to Rome, and I was requested to be present.

It is probably no exaggeration to state that Queen Margherita was, perhaps, the best loved of all the Italian royalties ; and Mussolini's ingenious arrangements on this sad occasion deserve great admiration. They were the triumph of Fascist organisation, and disciplined thoroughness.

The Royal train from Bordighera to Rome was

scheduled to do the journey in eighteen hours, that is at walking pace—a feat which must have imposed terrific strain on the locomotives, their drivers, and all the " personnel " on that line. During the whole of that time the route was entirely closed to other railway traffic, the ordinary trains having to be diverted in other directions ; an alteration which must have caused much additional work and great anxiety at the railway headquarters.

Exactly one minute in advance of the train, proceeding at a crawl, was a solitary " pilot " engine. Clockwork punctuality was maintained throughout that last, long, sad journey.

At one minute to seven, in the evening, the pilot engine drew into the Rapallo Station and halted. It was a mass of marguerites and palms. Punctually at seven o'clock the Royal train arrived at Rapallo and stopped. The locomotive, like the pilot engine, was wreathed in marguerites and palms. Immediately behind it was a coach, with blinds drawn, which contained the relief staff for the train. Next came the coach which carried the Royal coffin. The coach had been specially provided with glass sides, in order that all along the route, might see its interior, with the coffin, draped with the Italian flag, and an altar at which relays of priests read Mass. In all there were five coaches ; the third contained priests, the fifth wreaths. The fourth coach, which bore the Royal arms, contained Royal mourners and relatives of the Queen. Its blinds were drawn.

The train stopped for precisely one minute at each station along the route. There were no sounds during the halts ; the train left again on its journey without audible signals.

All the stations, big and small from Bordighera to Rome, were decorated with every flower that could be picked, from the choicest flower of the green-houses to the simple flowers that clustered on the mountain sides. Every lamp was covered in crape. At Genoa the whole station was draped in purple with crape hangings, and the Royal arms ; and an improvised altar was put up on the platform, alongside which the train drew up. On its arrival, Mass was said at this altar ; the station was thronged with people and there was hardly a dry eye to be seen as the last coach slowly disappeared.

Only one little station, in fact just a "halt" which consisted of a small wooden platform with a shelter, had no flowers. They were not easy to obtain there, on this rugged cliff near Rapallo, and the "halt" had been merely erected for the local fishermen's convenience for the transport of the fish. But the fisher-folk, who loved their Queen as much as others, showed their devotion and grief by giving all that meant most to them. Hanging from the shelter and lying on the platform were all sorts of fish ; their best haul of the day, and they knelt there with their empty baskets as the train steamed by. They had given all they had.

On the Apennine hills, at the foot of which the railway winds and bends, could be seen during the whole night the flickering light of the shepherds' torches and, many miles away, their horns could be heard giving their last salute.

CHAPTER X

ROMANCE continued to be popular in London as well as in Paris, and in October, 1926, this successful play was revived at the Playhouse, with Doris Keane again in the leading rôle. Unfortunately, Miss Keane at this time suffered a good deal in health, and it fell on me, as her understudy, to play her part on many occasions. On the first evening that I was called upon to act " Cavallini," I telephoned to my home in order to let the child's nurse know that I should be back later than usual.

When I returned after the performance, I was surprised to find the lights of the flat still burning.

I let myself in and found André in the process of undressing to go to bed. As he was just recovering from one of his innumerable attacks of bronchitis, I naturally strongly discountenanced " sitting up," and demanded an explanation. It was then revealed that he had been to the theatre to see me act. Apparently André had persuaded his nurse that it might be the only occasion on which I acted in the lead ; and on no account did he wish to miss the performance. After much debating and many entreaties, Nurse decided to risk it, and they went to the theatre. André sat in the upper circle with hot water-bottles strapped to his chest and back. As he moved the hot water-bottles emitted gurgling sounds, no doubt causing immediate neighbours to attribute them to a hurriedly consumed dinner with resulting indigestion.

At the end of the performance André was smuggled home ; and fortunately took no harm as the result of his night excursion.

In the middle of June, 1927, in reply to an invitation from M. Rozenberg, I went on a flying visit to Paris, and with him and his wife, Madeleine Soria, left for Vichy, where we gave a single performance of *Romance* at the Grand Casino.

A few weeks later, in August, Doris Keane took *Romance* on tour in the provinces. I was one of the company, and we went to Blackpool, Manchester, Edinburgh, and Glasgow. In each of those cities we spent a week.

At this time I seemed to be spending much of my life between London and Paris. In the late autumn I was again in the French capital. I was in three plays with the Stirlings and then resumed my association with that hardy annual *Romance* at the Théâtre Athenee. That revival lasted until March, 1929.

One evening as I was journeying by the Paris Underground on my way to the theatre, I unconsciously made a play upon words, which caused a great deal of amusement to my fellow-travellers. I was reading a newspaper and had found something which particularly interested me. But, as people who are familiar with Paris are aware, the illumination in the " Metro " is extremely poor, and so in order to see better I leant forward. I was wearing, as usual, a coat and skirt, and a blouse with a " V " neck. I suppose that in leaning forward one could

From an engraving

PUBLIC LETTER WRITER

see more of my neck than was considered proper.
I should have known nothing about this, but for
the fact that opposite me was a priest. I heard
some muttering and caught some remark about
manque de modestie, which caused me to look up.
I saw that the speaker was the priest. I gazed at
him, and all around me, to see what his trouble was,
hoping that something exceptionally exciting was to
be seen in our carriage ! " *C'est à vous, Madame, que
je parle ; vous êtes indecente. Vous montrez tous vos
seins !* " said he angrily to me. I so resented the
interruption of my reading for nothing at all, that I
indignantly retorted : " *Occupez vous de vos saints
au paradis, et laissez en paix les miens !* "

All within earshot burst into laughter and the
priest, who had turned as red as a beetroot, hastily
scrambled out at the next station. It was not until
a few minutes later that I realised what I had said,
and the point of the humour.

Coincidences are very curious things which make
one realise what strong psychological forces surround
one, and work their way, unknown to us. " Too
strange not to be true " is indeed a fact, and has
happened to myself more than once in my life.

During this time I had some very great friends in
Paris, Mr. and Mrs. " Z," who were very fond of me,
and of whom I saw a great deal. They were extremely
anxious that I should marry again, as they thought,
and with reason, that I should be happier with a
home and somebody to take care of André and me.
They had a great friend, a widower, and were always
telling me how well we should suit each other, as
our tastes were similar. They were only waiting
for an opportunity to enable us to meet. But he

o

lived in Brussels, and although he often came to Paris, it generally happened that I was not there at the same time. And so we never met.

On one of my trips, London–Paris, as I got into the train at Calais, I struggled in vain to close one of the windows before I sat down. The only other passenger in my compartment was a man. On seeing my difficulty he immediately rose, and very politely asked me to allow him to do it. We soon entered into conversation and by the time the train had reached Amiens we had become quite confidential. He was a good-looking middle-aged man, and obviously a man of culture who had travelled a lot. In talking of one thing and another, he told me he had some friends who were very anxious for him to marry again, and they had in their eye a very charming widow whom they knew very well. He also told me that he did not feel inclined to marry again, and that he had a very deep attachment in his life, of which he had never told his friends because he considered his private life only concerned himself. Eagerly I replied that I was entirely of his opinion. I then added that I too had some well-meaning friends who never ceased urging me to marry again, and to a friend of theirs.

We sympathised with each other about the interference of friends, and we went on to talk of other subjects.

By the time we arrived in Paris at the Gare du Nord we might have known each other for a long time, but . . . strange as it may seem, neither of us had exchanged names.

Mr. and Mrs. " Z," knowing that I was arriving,

had invited me to dinner that same night. When I entered their drawing-room, to my intense astonishment, there was my friend of the train! He was even more taken aback than myself, if such a thing was possible. Needless to say we stuck to our opinions, and the marriage did not come off!

I heard from these same friends the other day that my " travelling companion " is still a widower.

Talking of travelling backwards and forwards, reminds me of the great bus strike which happened in London some years ago. I was acting in London at the time and it was my matinée day. Walking towards the theatre with a friend, I happened to look at the clock in Oxford Street, and to my horror, saw that I had very little time to get to the theatre. To come to the aid of the public, and, incidentally, to make a penny or two, some of the men with initiative, had hired coal-carts to transport people to Piccadilly and other places. I was fortunate enough at that moment to catch sight of one of these coal-carts ; it was filled with chairs, but alas! every chair was occupied! Still, this mattered little to me, as I was in a desperate hurry, and with a leap and a bound I caught on to the back of it! A fat old woman with a basket and a small boy caught me by the arms and hauled me in. And my friend told me that the last she saw of me were two legs waving frantically in the air.

When next in Paris, I met the authoress, G. B. Stern, through her sister, May Malden, a great friend of mine ; and they introduced me to Frank Vernon and his wife, Virginia, who were going to produce the authoress's *Matriarch.* They offered me the part of " Aunt Elsa " and also the job of understudying Mrs. Patrick Campbell's rôle in the play. I am grateful to say that I was never called upon to deputise for the great actress. I have always enjoyed plenty of confidence and faith in my own ability, but I felt nervous at the idea of ever having to play that part.

The Matriarch began its career at the Royalty Theatre in the early days of May, 1929.

I became on very friendly terms with Mrs. Pat Campbell and often went home with her after the performance, and we used to sit talking till dawn. Mrs. Campbell is a woman of many interests, and her ability as a conversationalist is only exceeded by her brilliance as an actress. One day in her dressing-room in speaking of the altered conditions of the stage, she lamented the fact that modern actresses rarely receive a thorough training, rarely " go through the mill," as they did in the past. She then suddenly asked me if I remembered the play *Pelleas and Melisande,* and whether I had seen Sarah Bernhardt and herself in it. I told her I had. Mrs. Campbell then stood up and went through the whole of one of the acts of the play, taking on the parts of two people. It was one of the most remarkable and powerful exhibitions of acting that I have ever witnessed : it was spell-binding. The great actress seemed in acting to undergo a kind of transfiguration. The energy and vitality which she displayed were astounding. When she had finished the act, she sank into her chair.

" It's dreadful to realise that one is no longer young," she said to me.

In the last act of *The Matriarch,* Mrs. Patrick Campbell went on at the beginning for just a few minutes, and then had a fairly long wait before making her last appearance. I was, as I have stated, her understudy. In the theatre it is understood that understudies remain until their principal has made her last entrance. But it occurred to me that, in this case, it would be quite safe to leave after I had seen Mrs. Campbell make her first entrance in the last act. And so one day I asked her whether there was any necessity for me to wait till the end. Mrs. Campbell thought that there was no necessity. Undoubtedly, I should have made it my business to obtain official permission from the Stage Manager, but I considered Mrs. Campbell's agreement was sufficient, and I used to leave before the end . . . without the official consent of the proper authority.

One evening, during the long wait in the last act, Mrs. Campbell was, as usual, in her dressing-room. In making some movement she dislodged an electric fan which, in falling, made a severe gash on her shoulder. Mrs. Campbell at once called her dresser.

" Where is Elsa ? " she asked. " I can't finish the play ; she must go on with the part."

She was told that I had already left the theatre. Mrs. Campbell then very courageously asked for a stiff brandy and had her shoulder bandaged. She then went on to the stage and finished the play ; having forbidden those who knew about her accident to mention it, for fear that I should get into trouble if it were found out that I had left. The next night I naturally heard from my colleagues of the unfortunate incident and realised, for the first time, the gravity of my offence in not consulting the Stage Manager. However, Mrs. Campbell was sporting enough to have the matter kept a secret, to save me from the possibility of unpleasant consequences.

The Matriarch's run lasted until November, 1929, and then there occurred one of those inevitable pauses which most actresses experience at various times in their career.

I wrote to various managers, but, alas! there were no parts for me at the moment; so much of my time was spent at home looking after the house.

My maid one day asked me if I would order her a new broom as she was sadly in need of one, having just broken the handle of the long one she always used. I telephoned to a shop near us, asking them to send one at once; they replied they couldn't deliver till the next day. So, impatient as usual, I put my hat on and went to get it myself. I bought it and added to my collection a pail which I thought would be useful in the house. Much to the amusement of the shopkeeper, I insisted on carrying these articles home myself. And with the broom over my shoulder and the pail in my hand, I walked up Baker Street. To my dismay I suddenly came face to face with one of the managers I had written to, and knew only very slightly. He seemed astonished at my equipment, and asked me what I was doing; I replied that not having any work in view, I was going out charring! He laughed and passed on—and some time after offered me a part.

During this time, my boy was at school in Switzerland at Coppet, near Geneva, where I had sent him for the sake of his health. As I was free, I thought it was a good opportunity to go and see how he was getting on. I had not been to Geneva since the days I was there with my father: it seemed strange to be there in such different circumstances, and I thought with what pride he would have liked to be walking round the lake with his grandson.

The town itself had not changed much, so I easily found my way to the old " Brauerei " where Papa used to take me with him for the afternoon *goûter*, and now I in my turn was taking my child.

Unhappily, all my father's friends had now passed on.

It was very interesting for me to hear the many languages spoken in the streets as, although Geneva was always a very cosmopolitan town, it is all the more so now, since it has been the home of the League of Nations.

The school André was at, was called La Chataigneraie, and kept by an extremely nice man called Schartz-Buys. It is one of the most modern schools, and boys are sent there from America as well as from various other countries. The school has its own farm, therefore the boys get excellent food.

Each morning they are turned out into the grounds of the school at 6.30—winter and summer—for an hour's exercise before beginning the day.

It did André all the good in the world, and as well as speaking French, he now began to acquire some German.

I enjoyed my little visit there and then I returned home.

Apart from a revival of *The Outsider* in October, 1930, I had little to do with the theatre until 1931. I spent much of my free time in Paris.

After a time, I was again in a play by G. B. Stern, *Five Farthings*. It was produced at the Haymarket

Theatre with Marie Tempest in the leading rôle. My part, an amusing one, was that of an Italian manageress of a *pension* on the Riviera. I very much enjoyed my association with Marie Tempest who throughout, treated me with great kindness and consideration. This I particularly appreciated, for during the play I suffered great pain from an affection in one ear, and although the pain was considerably eased by special treatment it remained tender. Miss Tempest had, during one of the acts, to give me a playful little slap on the face, which certainly did not help to make the ear any better. But after some time, Miss Tempest apparently got to know about it, and she scolded me gently for keeping quiet about it. It would have been perfectly simple, she said, for her to have pretended to slap my face without actually striking it. I murmured something about not wishing to cause trouble. " Pluck can be carried to extremely foolish lengths," said Marie Tempest.

I was terribly sorry when the play ended, for Miss Tempest's personality and vitality are quite unique, and she gives such a human touch to all she does.

One does not wonder she is such a tremendous favourite with the British public.

In the autumn I found myself still at the Haymarket, but now in a play with the strange title of *Take Two From One.* Gertrude Lawrence and Peggy Ashcroft played the leads, and as a great many will remember, the late Horace Watson was the manager of the theatre—and a most dearly loved one.

Gertrude Lawrence loved practical jokes, and on one night selected her colleagues as the victims of her humour.

We had been called for the first act, and in passing her dressing-room were startled by what appeared to be an angry scene. Gertrude Lawrence, in a loud voice, was anouncing—to Horace Watson, as we assumed—her intention of striking, there and then, and of leaving the theatre. The whole cast gathered in a bunch behind the stage and began excitedly to discuss the " crisis."

We were about to fear the worst when Gertrude Lawrence herself, laughing heartily, ran towards us and said she had enjoyed her joke against us, and told us that there had been nobody but herself in the dressing-room ! We all felt much relieved.

1932, from my point of view, was a " scrappy " year. In January I paid a rush visit to Paris and took part in five special performances of *Romance*, still a great favourite with Parisian play-goers. I was also in several films, but in October again returned to the stage. It was not a particularly successful return, for the play in question, *Cold Blood*, was given a cold reception. It was produced at the Duke of York's, struggled on for a fortnight, and then fizzled out.

To console myself, because of the failure of *Cold Blood*, I decided to go and spend the Christmas holidays with my son and a friend of mine, in the South of France. I had a little Ford car at the time, so I planned to have a very pleasant journey in a kind of *dolce far niente* attitude, and not having to be in the continual tension of catching and missing trains. I also made up my mind to arrange our various halts so that we should arrive at les Baux for midnight Mass on Christmas Eve. Les Baux was an important town and stronghold, on the top of a mountainous rock, in the Middle Ages. It is in Provence, not far from Arles and Nimes. The most beautiful architectural ruins are to be seen there, and one has a most curious feeling, as one walks in and out of the empty houses, that the spirits of the people who once lived there still linger in those rooms. As one looks at the wonderful fireplace of the Hôtel de Manville, one feels that a huge fire should be roaring up the chimney. Most impressive also is the steeple of the church which used to be called " the lantern of the dead " because in the Middle Ages, when some important personage was dying, a lighted lantern was placed inside the steeple which was specially constructed for this purpose, and in such a way that the dim light could be seen from every part of the town, and that the inhabitants could, therefore, pray for the departing soul.

Les Baux is now a dead city ; only two hundred and one inhabitants were left, when I was there last. The only flicker of life it seems to have is its Midnight Mass on Christmas Eve. People of all sorts and descriptions, from the rich man in his car, to the shepherd on the hill, come to this charming ceremony which carries us back to five hundred years ago. Shepherds, with their crooks, sing all the Christmas carols in the Provençial dialect, whilst the children, dressed as angels, lead into the church a tiny cart all beribboned and lit by candles and inside which is a baby lamb.

Having timed the journey as I wanted to, it was ten o'clock at night when we began our drive up the bare, rocky mountains. It is difficult for me to express in words the beauty of that starry night, and the dreamlike effect of the lights of the cars

ihead of us, as they zigzagged round the bends
of the mountain.

When we reached the town we found it already
full of people, and the church so crowded that we
each had to make our own way as we could, and so
we got separated. Mass began, and I was becoming
more and more squashed, by an ever-increasing flow
of humanity ; but I was so anxious as to what
fate had befallen my son and my friend, that I
forgot that I was being slowly but surely suffocated.
At last, in a desperate effort to breathe, I jerked
my head upwards, raised my eyes and saw, to my
extreme surprise, both my travelling companions
comfortably seated on chairs in the organ loft, where,
through sheer perseverance they had pushed their
way !

Gianandrea and I spent the Easter holidays, 1933,
in Rome. It was his first visit there. His school,
and various illnesses, and my stage work had made
it impossible for us to go there together before. It
was a new and thrilling pleasure for me to take
him around not only to see all my friends, but all
the places full of my childhood and girlhood memories.
As one of the postal motor vans tore past us, in
Via del Babuino, I told him of how, when the horse
vans were done away with and the first bright
yellow motor vans appeared, and speeded like
lightning through the narrow streets of Rome, they
had been called, *Il pericolo giallo* (the yellow peril).
They were nicknamed thus, because it was the time
when all Europe's politicians were getting alarmed
at the preponderance of China and Japan's importance, and all the newspapers were full of the
menacing dangers of Eastern yellow peril.

This nickname was the cause of an amusing and rather touching incident. One of these *pericoli giallo* nearly knocked my father down one day at the corner of a street. My cousin Giuseppe Vitelleschi was going to Repasto for a week-end to see his brother-in-law, Giuseppe Serafini, who was already there. On arriving he said to the latter, in the hearing of one of our peasants : " Just fancy, Zio Checco (Uncle Checco) was nearly killed by a *pericolo giallo*." The very next day whilst we were at lunch at Palazzo Massimo, the butler announced that " Vecchi " the overseer had called to ask news of my father to whom he was most anxious to speak. The old man was naturally shown in at once, and twisting his old shepherd's felt hat nervously in his hands, he looked at my father with the expression of a faithful devoted dog, and big tears dropped down his rugged, wrinkled cheek as he said : " Master, let me go and kill him. We cannot lose you." Papa gazed at him in astonishment and enquired the reason of this astounding proposition, and who was the prospective victim. Vecchi's face became ferocious as he hissed out between clenched teeth : " That horrible Oriental who tried to kill you the other day." My father was much touched by the man's devotion, and took him out to show him what was called the *pericolo giallo* in Rome.

When gazing up at Palazzo Massimo from Piazza dell' Ara Coeli (meaning Altar of Heaven) so called on account of the church of the same name which stands at the foot of the Capitol, I was showing Gianandrea the windows of our flat, explaining to him the position of each room. This reminded me of a few more incidents of my old life, and I smiled in recalling the little exclamation of surprise and indignation, which came from my Aunt Clotilde, the beautiful Spanish wife of Papa's brother Giulio, when on one occasion when she came to see Mama, she sat on a valuable high-backed chair on which I had inadvertently left my doll's dress which I was sewing, with the needle sticking up. That particular week was a week of calamities, as the very next morning whilst dusting the drawing-room, the footman, whose task it was in Rome, put on the floor various china ornaments amongst which a most precious antique Sèvres tray with two cups and saucers, coffee pot and sugar basin. The front-door bell suddenly rang, and the footman in going to answer it, put his foot right into the middle of the tray ! I can well remember his consternation and my mother's grief, as this set was a particular favourite of hers. But such was her consideration for the feelings of others, that when this wretched man in a dithering condition went to inform her of the catastrophe, the only comment she made was: " It would have been worse if you had lost a leg."

I walked up the Capitol steps with my son and showed him the wolves in their cages, reminding him of the legend of Romulus and Remus ; I likewise pointed out to him the big cage where sits a beautiful specimen of an eagle in memory of the Roman Empire of the Cæsars, and then we walked into the Campidoglio itself, where, in silence, we stood in front of the marble bust of my father.

The old white-haired custodian, seeing us standing there motionless, came up and looked at us enquiringly. I explained to him who we were ; upon which, this old man who had been there for the last forty years, was so overcome that the tears poured down his cheeks as he approached my son and reverently kissed him on each shoulder, murmuring as he did so : " God has given me the honour of seeing the grandson of that great man."

I left the Capitol with a very sad heart, as it brought back to me so vividly all my happy youth ; but at the same time I was touched and pleased to see how the memory of my father is still alive to-day.

It seems to me only yesterday when my mother arrived in Rome one evening with her maid and all her trunks. The next night she was going with my father to a great reception at the British Embassy.

The following morning the whole house was roused ; Mama's maid had informed her that on unpacking the trunk which contained her jewel-case, she had found the said case completely empty ; every single jewel had gone.

The Chief of Police was called in at once, and after a minute examination he expressed the opinion that the jewels had never left London. Unhappily, in those days, English women had the habit of packing their jewels in their trunks, and very few of them even insured them. My mother was amongst these, and the loss of her jewels amounted to thousands of pounds.

The Rome police immediately communicated with Scotland Yard, who informed us that the day before my mother left London, the maid had sent to her brother in America, a sealed package. This brother had been twice in prison for theft. Everything pointed to her being the thief, but we could not bring a direct accusation against her. Naturally we gave her notice at once.

Notwithstanding the loss of the jewels, my mother went to the Embassy party that night; and I remember how beautiful she looked when, just before going out, dressed in a lovely but simple white satin dress, covered by her red plush cloak with collar and lining of white Persian lamb, she smiled sweetly, and in saying " Good night " to me she pinned on the yoke of my dress the only jewel she had left—a little diamond and pearl brooch in the shape of a marguerite, which she had worn on the journey.

Somehow she seemed to me even more lovely without jewels.

The next day she took me with her to the well-known Villa Celimontana near the Coliseum, whose grounds were literally a carpet of violets, and their scent wafted towards us as we approached.

Mama adored flowers and as we walked about amongst them she suddenly said : " They are far more beautiful than jewels."

As Gianandrea and I were rushing to the Allievi for lunch one day, it reminded me of another occasion, when equally I was late, many years before my son's birth, and in the days when one wore big leghorn hats trimmed with flowers. I was tearing along the pavement, when a dirty little street urchin aged about six, planted himself in front of me, with both his hands in his torn pockets. In my haste I nearly fell over him ; he still did not move. " Well, what's the matter with you ? " I said, somewhat irritably.

" I wanted to see if you were there under that big hat," was the impudent reply, and he rushed off before I could answer him adequately.

But now I really must stop all these Roman

reminiscences . . . yet not without adding *one*, which was a most happy one for the person concerned. I will first of all explain for those who do not know, what the " Gioco del Lotto " in Italy is. Many tourists have probably passed by, time after time in Italian streets, these little offices over the doors of which are placards with the words " Gioco del Lotto " (game of lottery). It is a Government lottery, but quite different to any others, and so much is it in the blood of the people that, were it done away with, I feel confident it would cause a revolt. Every Saturday, numbers are drawn in the principal square of the big Italian towns, and the evening papers give the lucky numbers.

Italians are by nature very superstitious, and believers in the occult and mysticism ; they have always been so, as history proves, going back as far as 715 B.C., when Numa Pompilius consulted the nymph Egeria and asked her to explain to him the meaning of his dreams. Tarquin the Proud equally based his life on the forecasts and predictions of the famous Cumæn sybil, whose reputation is still world-famed to-day.

To choose the numbers, the modern Italian gambles with, he selects them from the " dream book " in which one finds numbers corresponding with every kind of dream ; so according to his dream he chooses his numbers. I remember a few of them, such as : Fear is 90 ; dead man who speaks is 47 ; woman's legs 88 !

One of our maids, when I was a child, came to my mother delirious with joy one Saturday evening. She had had a dream whose numbers worked out to be 33—27—5, and she had won ! Three numbers coming out thus in succession meant winning *un terno* (three numbers) and a huge sum of money, 500,000 lire, which meant thousands of pounds. She is now a rich woman, and the other day in Rome, when I was in a bus, I saw her lounging back comfortably in a big Isotta car! Dreams come true!

On our return we stopped in Paris, but not in the manner I had anticipated. We had taken our places in the Rome–Paris Express, and I asked André to put one of the suit-cases on the rack, which he did. Subsequently he complained of an internal pain. On reaching Paris I took him to see the famous surgeon, de Martel, a very great friend of ours. De Martel's diagnosis revealed appendicitis in a mild form. A simple operation, quickly performed, would set him right again.

The operation lasted two and a half hours, and but for Dr. de Martel's skill would have proved fatal. André remained in the nursing-home for six weeks.

While he was recovering, I was operated upon next door . . . for appendicitis, also!

As soon as we were in a fit state to travel we came back to London, and I sent André to stay with a professor and his wife at Burgess Hill to recuperate. Foolishly, he climbed over a wall and fell, thus re-opening the wound, and back he came to London for treatment.

In September, after the summer holidays, he seemed quite fit and returned as usual to Wellington College ; so I thought that at last all was doing well.

During November I accepted a film engagement

P

at Twickenham, and on the night before I was
starting my first day's work at the studios, I retired
early to bed in order to be as fresh as possible for
the next morning. After I had been asleep for some
while, I was suddenly awakened by the telephone.
Mrs. Trevelyan, wife of André's house-master, was
speaking from the college. He had been taken
suddenly very ill, and they had motored him to a
nursing-home in Reading. She asked me to come
down at once. I jumped out of bed, dressed hurriedly
and caught the last train from Paddington Station.
On arriving at Reading I went at once to the
nursing-home, where it was reported to me that an
operation for blood-poisoning had been found
necessary. The surgeon then told me that he feared
the presence of a particular germ, in which case
there would be little hope for the patient. However,
it would not be possible to discover this until forty-
eight hours had passed. But as I was expected at
the film studios for an early start at seven in the
morning, and as the company would have no chance
at such short notice, of procuring a substitute for
me, I had to do my best to be at Twickenham
punctually. Moreover, the surgeon assured me that
I could serve no good purpose in remaining at the
hospital. The Matron and the doctors were extremely
kind to me and very sympathetic, and I knew that
the best attention would be given to my son.

I was brought some food and hot coffee, which
the nurse insisted on my taking, after which the
Matron made me lie on a sofa before the drawing-
room fire, all warmly tucked in blankets, where I
remained until I left by the five-something train
from Reading, and reached the studio in time.

My days were spent in film work, the nights in travelling to and from Reading. During the whole time I existed in a state of cruel uncertainty. I could not eat much, but kept myself going with black coffee ; I felt I was at the end of all things.

As good fortune would have it, the doctor's fears proved to be unfounded ; the dreaded germ was not present. Still, three further operations were necessary before the patient was pronounced free of the poison. Whether he would recover, said the doctor, depended on the ability of his constitution to overcome the horrible weakness with which the ordeal had left him. The waiting and anxiety of those days were the most dreadful sensations that I have ever experienced. Slowly, however, André began to mend, and about Christmas time he was able to leave for Switzerland to recuperate. I had made arrangements with his old schoolmaster at Coppet to take him temporarily.

I can never forget the great and exceptional kindness of André's house-master at Wellington College, Mr. Trevelyan. He could not have done more, even for his own child ; no trouble was too much for him, and he himself motored André into Reading the night he was taken ill, came to fetch me at the station when I arrived, past midnight, and stayed with me at the nursing home until three in the morning, and this after a hard day's work.

Just prior to this crisis I had received a letter from Francis de Croisset, who wrote to tell me that *Romance* was to be produced at the Odeon in Paris, that is at the French State Theatre. He was very anxious that I should play my old part as he could obtain the consent of the Government to my inclusion in the State Troupe, an honour which foreigners seldom, if ever I believe, obtain. I immediately replied enthusiastically in the affirmative. M. de Croisset secured the three permits which I required : the permit of residence, the permit to work in France, and—the most difficult to obtain—the permit to join the French State Theatre Company. And so I became a pensionnaire of the Odeon, the second State Theatre of France.

I left for Paris in the middle of December. André on his way to Switzerland to convalesce passed through, and I saw him for the first time since his recovery ; he was looking very pale and bloodless, but I had implicit faith in the Swiss air, which I knew would benefit him greatly.

My admission to the French State Company was a unique event, and brought me a great deal of publicity through the French Press. The fact was brought home to me in a rather strange manner.

I had bought a midday paper, the *Paris Midi*, and without opening it jumped on to a motor bus, intending to read it when I arrived home. After some while I grew conscious that my neighbour, a gentleman, was paying me a considerable amount of notice. Out of the corner of my eye I saw that he alternatively glanced at his paper and at me. That he continued to do for some time until I grew really embarrassed. I sought refuge behind my newspaper. On opening it, I discovered on the centre page a portrait of myself and about half a page of description. I gasped and turned to look

at my neighbour. He was reading the same newspaper; and now, having seen me full-face, felt
satisfied that he recognised me.

" *C'est bien vous, Madame,*" he said.

I admitted it, in a rather flustered way, as I had
not been prepared for so much advertisement.

My neighbour in the bus then told me that he had
seen me in the play and that he had greatly enjoyed
the acting and the story. He wished me success
and that I should have many more chances of being
seen on the Paris stage.

Subsequently I discovered the whole of my life-
story had made its way into all the French newspapers.

The next evening on arriving at the theatre, I
noticed that about twenty people were crowded
round the stage door, and the concierge was
trying to send them away by saying : " *Je vous dit
qu'elle est deja en train de se maquiller et elle ne peut
voir personne.*" (I tell you she is already making up
and can see nobody.) I naturally thought they were
waiting to see Madeleine Soria. I pushed my way
through and went up to my dressing-room. Shortly
after, the concierge came upstairs and told me that
all those people were workers of the Italian colony in
Paris who, having read all about me in the papers,
had come to the theatre to see their fellow-country-
woman, and wanted to speak to her ! He added
that he thought one or two of them wanted not only
the privilege of speaking to me, but also the honour
of being helped ! As they were bent on returning
at the end of the performance, he advised me to go
out by the front of the house.

I remained at the Odeon until the end of April,

1934, when the play was taken off, much to my sorrow, as I loved being there.

The number of performances of *Romance* I have taken part in, both in London and Paris have now reached 2197 !

Before returning to London I had a conversation with Francis de Croisset, who again congratulated me, as my having played at the Odeon, he said, would firmly establish my position in the theatre world, not only in France, but in England also. In London, in future, only leading parts would be offered me— that was the conviction of M. de Croisset.

Not long afterwards, I met in one of the London streets a well-known personage of the theatre. I told him that I was just back from Paris, and of my association with the Odeon. I added confidently that I was now waiting for someone to come along with a splendid offer. From now on I expected only leading parts, I said.

" What makes you think that ? " asked the man of the theatre. " Just because you have acted at the Odeon Cinema ? "

My enthusiasm immediately ebbed. I realised now that the Odeon meant nothing in London, even if people were sufficiently well informed to know that it stood for the French State Theatre, and not a cinema, as some people seemed to imagine. What I had done in France would have no effect on my position in England.

But at this time I badly needed an engagement. If there was no leading part for me, I was prepared to accept gratefully the smallest of parts. The long chapter of illness, and the many operations which my son had undergone, had made serious inroads in my finances ; and at the time of which I am writing I was in great difficulties.

When things were beginning to look very black, Gilbert Miller nobly came to the rescue, and through him I was kept steadily in work from June, 1934, to June, 1936—in *Men in White* and *Tovarich*, both of which were at the Lyric Theatre. With that my immediate worries were removed. Dreams of leading parts seemed to have vanished more than ever : but far from being ungrateful, I was glad of those parts, small as they were.

It was during the run of *Men in White* that my boy had to undergo another operation. Dr. de Martel in Paris, whom I am fortunate enough to have as a friend, very kindly offered to perform this operation, as he had done the first one for appendicitis, which had been most serious. I was told at the time that only Martel would have dared operate and succeed with the boy's appendix in such a state. Unquestionably he saved my son's life. Kindness such as his one rarely gets, and I shall never cease to think of him with gratitude.

As I said good-bye to my son at Victoria Station I felt rather sad and very worried ; but it was a great relief to me that he was going to stay two days, before entering the nursing home, with Countess Orietta Borromeo, who had most kindly put off leaving Paris for a few days as she knew that I could not give up my work.

As everybody will remember, *Men in White* was a play which portrayed entirely hospital life. The whole plot revolved round medical students, nurses, and doctors, and the big scene of the play was the operating theatre, with all the doctors and students preparing for a big operation. The proficiency of Gilbert Miller in having all his plays perfect, and accurate in every detail is well known.

Our rehearsals had been attended by the Matron and some of the surgeons of St. George's Hospital, so that every item should be correct.

In this play my part was that of an Italian widowed mother named Mrs. Andrea, whose only son had to have a severe operation performed on him. The scene where Mrs. Andrea implored the surgeons to save her son's life was most pathetic and dramatic. At the end of the play one heard that the son was saved. It seemed to me an odd fact that my part should be so much like my present circumstance, even to the name being Andrea.

To my great joy, de Martel rang me up from Paris immediately after the operation, to tell me that it had been most successful.

Three weeks later André returned to England, and went to the Agricultural College of Seale Hayne at Newton Abbot, where the good food and Devonshire air soon built him up. So much did he like the college and the work, that it gave him the idea of becoming a veterinary surgeon, and it was from there he entered as a student the Veterinary College in Edinburgh.

The " Depression " moved on when, in July, 1936, Auriol Lee, whom I had known very well for many years, and who has always been most kind to me, offered me a beautiful part in *The Lady of La Paz*, in which I had plenty of scope for acting. We opened at the Criterion Theatre.

It was the first time in my career that I had met

Lilian Braithwaite, from whom I learnt so much, and who gave me great help. I realised that her exceptional ability lies not only in her subtle and delicate acting, but in her gift of making others on the stage live their parts.

CHAPTER XI

January, 1937

I AM writing this last chapter in the train on my way back to London from Lamington, Scotland, where I have been spending the week-end with my uncle, Lord Lamington. During this visit the memories of my childhood were more vividly recalled than on any of the previous ones ; the reason being, no doubt, that in writing these memoirs lately the events and incidents of long ago were being strongly revived.

As I walked through the " Glen " and past the " Burn," I saw myself again as a small child in a white-embroidered frock and big brown holland pinafore, running along the paths, singing and laughing, with fun and glee.

My grandfather, the late Lord Lamington, had had the lovely idea of asking each important guest and each member of our family to plant a small fir tree near the Glen. There are but a few small trees now, the greater number are full-grown. Some, alas, are the only living memory of very dear ones who have passed into the Great Beyond !

Disraeli's tree is at the very beginning of the Glen ; he planted it in 1873. Mine is also among the grown-ups now.

All the trees are labelled with the names of the persons who planted them and the date.

Over the porch of the house, my grandfather had engraved the following words :

Pax entrantibus
Salus exeuntibus
Benedictio habitantibus.

meaning :

Peace to those who enter
Godspeed to those who leave
Blessing to those who dwell here.

My uncle very kindly asked my son over for the week-end so that we should be together. André is studying in Edinburgh, and he is always delighted to visit Lamington, as he is very fond of the place, and of hearing from the old butler, stories of what I used to do as a little girl. The one he particularly enjoys is how, when I was five or six, on arriving at Lamington, I used invariably to run into the hall and curtsey to the butler !

In the private Chapel of the family, which is in the grounds at the end of the park, rests in peace all that is earthly of my grandfather and grandmother, Alexander and Annabella, first Lord and Lady Lamington, of my dearly loved mother and of my aunt, Constance, Countess Delaware, and I thought with sorrow of how quickly the years pass, and those whom we love pass on.

In the days when I was a little child, the Chapel only saw services of joy and thanksgiving ; those who now lie at rest in it, were full of life and hopes. Their memory has not been allowed to fade ; every day

November 27 :/73

Dear Amy:

You may
depend upon
my all forgetting'
yours

from wish, &c
whi: I am honored
& gratified — but
as you are already
your way to the
South I will

not astonish the
postmaster of
Baggar by sending
it thro' his auspices,
but it shall be
left at your home
in London, as
soon

DISRAELI'S LETTER TO THE AUTHOR'S MOTHER WHEN SHE
WAS A YOUNG GIRL.

fresh flowers are laid on their graves by the living members of the family.

I sometimes wonder how much those who have gone are able to see here ? At least, it is to be hoped, that they can behold the ultimate happiness which surely must come, after the great sorrows we go through.

I have such happy memories of my Aunt Contie (Countess De la Warr) and those days I spent at her country place, Inchmery, without a care in the world. Inchmery was a beauty spot in itself, situated on the Solent ; at high-tide the sea used to come up to the thick hedges that separated it from the lawn ; many hours did I spend basking in the sunshine on the shore when the tide was low, and watching the ocean liners as they drifted from Southampton past the Needles to the great sea beyond.

My aunt had a yacht then, the *Violet,* and she used to steam backwards and forwards to Cowes with the same " insouciance " as one takes a penny bus from Piccadilly to Oxford Circus, no matter what the weather was like. In fact, the rougher the sea, the more she enjoyed it ! The only trouble was that she insisted on obliging her guests going with her !

I remember one particular day, when the sea was iron grey with anger, and Aunt Contie insisted on going over to Cowes for lunch and taking with her the Princess Poggio Suasa and the latter's sister, the Marquise de Talleyrand, and Hamilton Gatliff. The three of them begged to be let off this " pleasure trip," but it was useless ! The crossing was dreadful ; the Princess and her sister lay below without moving, and Aunt Contie sat on the stern of the deck, where a lot of leather cushions had been placed, playing

Picquet with Hamilton Gatliff, who, luckily for him, was an excellent sailor. Whilst they were playing and arguing, and the yacht ploughing through the waves, a sudden gust of wind blew one of the cards into the sea. Aunt Contie cried out to the captain to stop at once ! The old captain, who had been with her for years, looked over the helm, his beard waving in the gale, and he said : " Don't be childish, my lady, one would hardly stop in a storm like this to save oneself."

Those who knew my aunt will recognise in this little story, her delicious impulsive childlike nature that believed that everything she wanted was humanly possible ; yet she was never bitter, or resentful when she could not obtain the impossible.

Another day my aunt was giving a big charity bazaar in the garden, and suddenly all the hens and ducks came hopping and cackling and flopping in the middle of everybody, making the most dreadful noise. Aunt Contie's son, Gilbert, had put whisky in their food, and then, when they were nicely drunk, he had shoo-ed them all on to the lawn !

So many amusing incidents occurred at Inchmery that it would need a whole volume to relate them all. It was a house where everybody felt at home, and as if they had been there for years. My aunt was the most unconventional, vivacious person I have ever met ; she had a great sense of humour and her *joie de vivre* knew no bounds. As from her early days, her daughter, Margaret Sackville, took to writing, there were also many literary people who came for week-ends to Inchmery. Amongst them, John Beith, who, as Ian Hay, is now one of the favourite authors of the day—and rightly so. He and I, who, for some providential reason, were left alone to do as we liked, used to have many a laugh together as we watched the unfortunate victims being led to the yacht like lambs to the slaughter ! It was impossible not to love Aunt Contie, she had a charm that was all her own.

And as I stood by my dear ones' graves at Lamington all these memories seemed to me so real ; it was nearly impossible for me to realise that their tangible existence had gone.

Fate seems to have decreed that, at a time when I am ending these memoirs, I should visit, within a few days of each other, the two birthplaces of my childhood memories, Rome and Lamington—Italy and Scotland.

Both Italian and Scottish blood flow in my veins ; Italy of the South, and Scotland of the North, are my two homes. Evidently I am the point at which extremes meet !

In analysing myself, I realise how fundamentally I have in me the characteristics of both these races, which, oddly enough, though they seem on the surface so very far apart, yet in their inner selves they possess many qualities which are common to both. They are both dreamers and inclined to mysticism, though outwardly it takes different forms. Probably it is owing to that, that the Italian in me, which I inherit from my father, lives on terms of peace with the Scottish in me, which I have from my mother.

I returned just a month ago from Rome, where I went to spend a fortnight's holiday with the friends of my childhood, whose welcome to me whenever I go there is always like a warm day of sunshine.

Most of them are married, and have children of about the same age as my son. My friends and I get together and talk over old times, which seem to us so vivid that, at moments, when we are suddenly interrupted by one of our offsprings asking : " But who is So and So ? " we answer, without thinking : " Don't be so silly, you remember quite well," forgetting for the instant that they were then neither born nor thought of ! And now one or two are already married, others are working for a career, and some have been out to the war in Abyssinia last year.

Manolo Borromeo, the son of my very dear friend, Orietta Doria Borromeo, used to write to me most interesting letters whilst he was there during the campaign, telling me also about a small motherless camel which he had adopted after one of the attacks, and that he had really hated leaving it. When I saw him in Rome the other day, he talked to me a lot about Abyssinia and its possibilities for cultivation and the wonderful way the campaign was organised with every forethought for the comfort of the troops.

At the moment everyone in Italy is, naturally, talking very much of Africa, of its future, its present, and its past, and all sorts of stories and incidents are told, one of which I must repeat. Many years ago, a missionary priest was sent out to convert some of the remote tribes in Central Africa. He baptised and brought many into the Church, but one of the chiefs had two wives, and when told he must give up one of them on becoming a Christian, he was somewhat upset, as he did not know which one to choose. However, the missionary baptised him on the condition that he would give up one of his wives. The priest told him he was going further on to another tribe and would be back in about a month. A month passed, the missionary returned and a great feast was celebrated in his honour, with all the native ceremonies. After the feast was over, the priest told the chief that he hoped the wife who had been given up had been well provded for. The chief smiled in a childlike way, and pointing to one of the big cauldrons he said : " Oh, yes, she is with God. When I decided which one to keep, I killed the other, and we have been eating her."

As I had lived in England for so long it was interesting to me to hear the Italian point of view on all these vital subjects of to-day.

Owing to my having been in continual work in London, first in *Tovarich*, which ran for over a year, and then straight on in *The Lady of La Paz*, I had not been able to go to Rome for the last two years.

Happily for me I still have two first cousins left in Rome, my father's nieces. One of them is the daughter of my uncle Giulio and his beautiful Spanish wife Clotilde. This cousin, whose name is Maria, is still a very handsome woman, although over seventy. In her youth she was one of the three most beautiful Roman society girls of the day. All three were called Maria and were known as *le tre bellissime Marie* (the three most beautiful Maries).

The other cousin is the daughter of my uncle Angelo and she still lives in the Palazzo Vitelleschi in Rome. As I go up the stairs to visit her I see in my mind's eye all those of my family who walked, and ran up and down, my father, and my uncles ; and the staircase seems haunted with the spirits of the Vitelleschis who have passed on. There is

always something tragic in thinking of the past;
it had been such a merry home and happy family.
The whole house used to ring at first with the laughter
of the numerous children of my grandparents, and
later with the shouts of glee of my cousins. Now,
of the elder branch, only three of us are left; and
strange to say, I am the only one of that elder branch
who was not born in our palazzo. This cousin who
lives in the palazzo is also called Maria, so to
distinguish her from the other cousin she has always
been known as Mariella. Her brother was Padre
Giovanni, the well-known Jesuit, whom I have
already mentioned. Their other sister Giulia had
married Rodolfo Kanzler, whose father had been
Colonel-in-Chief of the Swiss Guards at the Vatican,
where Rodolfo himself also had an important post.
He was the archæological authority of all the new
excavations of Ancient Rome and specially of the
Catacombs. It is to him one owes the discovery of
many ancient treasures. So great was his knowledge,
that on finding the smallest fragment of a stone he
could tell what it belonged to, and where it came
from. Many of the important early Christian tablets
which are seen to-day in the Catacombs were
reconstructed by him bit by bit until they were
well-nigh perfect. His death was a great loss to all
archæological research and a terrible grief to my
cousin Giulia, from which she never recovered. One
of her two sons, Angelo, was killed in the Great War;
he was only twenty and as handsome and good as
his name implies. These two tragedies shortened
Giulia's life, she lost all zest for living, and she died
from a broken heart. She combined in her the
greatest intelligence with the greatest charm; her

salons were amongst the most frequented in Rome. Her only surviving son Ermanno died a few years ago in the Palazzo Vitelleschi, and Mariella feels the loss of her nephew very deeply. Therefore it seems now that the younger branch of the family will come to the fore, as my cousin Pier Marcello, who is in the Consular Service, married a charming, beautiful Norwegian girl, and has three sons.

Undoubtedly, Rome has much changed from what it used to be when I was a child and looked out of my nursery window, which gave on to the Piazza Tor de Specchi (meaning Square of the Tower of Mirrors). This little square used to lead to the Temple of Vesta, and on the way, one passed through Piazza Montanara, the famous market-place where all the Roman peasants used to assemble.

In pulling down all the old houses in this neighbourhood to widen the streets these squares have disappeared ; and now, thanks to Mussolini, a lovely wide avenue goes direct from the Campidoglio to the Temple of Vesta.

Over and over again, I used to watch from my window the queues of servant girls and peasants lining up in the piazza, holding in their hands brilliant-coloured paper and envelopes, awaiting their turn to have their letters written by the *scrivano publico* (public letter-writer). He used to sit there on his rustic chair, at his ink-stained small wooden table, for hours and hours, writing letter after letter, and repeating out loud as he wrote each phrase that was being dictated to him. On rainy days he sat under a huge multi-coloured umbrella.

I remember being greatly thrilled one day to see amongst the crowd a little housemaid of ours who pushed everybody else aside, which caused much bickering and excited discussion ; but she won the day and arrived triumphantly at the " scrivano's " table. I realise now that she must have slipped out of the house without permission, and was terrified of being discovered!

Speaking of windows, leads me to another episode which happened, this time, at my mother's dressing-room window, which was close to my nursery. I happened to be with my mother whilst she was dressing to go out in the afternoon ; a barrel-organ was playing in the street below. As it was a warm afternoon the window was open, and my mother went to and fro to her bedroom. I was about seven at this time. She called out to me from the other room to take a penny from the dressing-table and throw it to the man. I looked for a penny but could not see one, so I took her pearl necklace, which lay on the table and which to me conveyed no value, and I flung it into the street ! The noise and excitement which ensued in the street attracted Mama's attention. She looked out and saw the man gazing up, and holding her necklace in his hands ! Needless to say, the necklace was retrieved and the man was made happy by getting far more than he would otherwise have done. But I was severely scolded, which upset me greatly, because I could not grasp the difference of value between a penny and a pearl !

The street was so narrow that, like some of the old streets in the City of London, not only could one carry on conversations quite comfortably with those who lived opposite, but with the aid of a stick one could also pass objects from one window to the opposite one. Many little bags of sweets were thus transferred to me by a very kind lady who lived opposite, and who had been governess to one of my cousins.

Rome, queen among cities, has weathered the stormy and difficult times of childhood, youth, the days of war, economic crises, and unexpected turmoils of the upheaval of Mother Europe in 1914, which changed the situation of our continent. The citizens, although they have had to alter their ways and mode of living in order to remain in harmony with modern times, have retained their typical characteristics and remain Romans.

As one walks down the streets in the poorer parts of Rome, one still hears to-day loving mothers calling from their windows to their children in the street below: " Hector! Juno! Ajax! Minerva!" and other names of ancient gods and goddesses; also the names of the poets Virgil, Ovid, Livy, and mixed with them the various titles of the Blessed Virgin, such as Assunta, Immacolata, Annunziata, and also names of saints.

Ever since Rome has existed the Romans have always been very familiar with Divinity; as much as in the days of the past when Janus was the god of the household door and principally worshipped by men, and Vesta was particularly favoured by women, as later when Rome became Christian. In the days of paganism they offered sacrifices of male animals to male deities and female animals to female deities. They even treated their gods according to their social position! White animals were offered to the gods of the upper world, and black animals to the gods below! Now they offer their jewels, their votive gifts, their candles to the saints, which are represented by statues and pictures in the churches. Some of the statues, such as the one of the Blessed Virgin in the church of Sant' Agostino in Rome, where expectant mothers go every day to pray for their safety in childbirth, is literally covered with jewels of all descriptions, including valuable diadems, worth thousands of pounds.

People of the North are full of awe towards God, and regard Divinity as something rather far away, whom they dare not approach except with the greatest reverence. Naturally, I am only generalising in saying this, for I know there are many who think differently. For the Southern races, and specially for the Italians, God is a loving friend, always near them, mixed up in their everyday life, and of whom they ask every necessity, great or small; and if these favours are not granted, they are quite capable of getting very annoyed with God, as they would with one of themselves who did not do what they wanted. Originally it was just an avalanche of reproaches, which, unhappily, degenerated into blasphemy that so much shocked and horrified everybody; though half the time the blasphemers did not even realise what they were saying; it was just a matter of habit in outbursts of ill temper. Mussolini has succeeded in completely eradicating blasphemy in all its forms. As far as the actual worshipping of God is concerned, one wonders if it is not more pleasing to Him to be treated as a loving, intimate friend, rather than as a great and powerful Authority. There is something very touching in the happy and familiar faith of the Italians, which is perhaps missing in the religion of the Northerners.

People have sometimes said to me that they were rather shocked at the private conversations held in Italian churches, and at seeing a young man kissing a young girl behind the ear whilst she is crossing herself with holy water. But the Italian considers the church as if it were his own home, and he were in the presence of a most loving, understanding Father, who takes an interest in everything His child does and is the first to rejoice if He sees him happy. No people have better understood the words of the psalmist : " *Servite Domino in lætitia* " (Serve the Lord with gladness) than the Italians. The word " Feast " has in Italy a significance of its own. All the religious commemorations, except those of Holy Week, are called *feste* (feast days), a word which expresses rejoicing and gladness, much more than piety. The days of obligation ordained by the church, on which all have to go to Mass, are in the Italian villages kept as a fête day, in which all the villagers, after having been to Mass in their Sunday clothes, go to the tavern to drink and enjoy themselves. The church bells ring out their joyous peal, and in the evening there is, even in the smallest village, a display of fireworks which always has a great fascination for the Italian people. One of the greatest religious attractions for not only Italians of all classes, but for the Roman Catholics of the whole world, is to see St. Peter's in Rome. For most, this feeling is in no way connected with its architectural splendour, historical importance, or the untold art treasures it contains. The cupola of Michelangelo represents for them a luminous beacon, showing them a safe harbour which shelters them from the dangerous currents of doubt and uncertainty, and from the tempest of passions which in a vast and rough sea make life's journey so difficult.

One of the things which makes Rome so uniquely interesting is the amalgamation of paganism and Christianity. Of the seven hills on which Rome is built, the Janiculum still bears its name given to it in honour of Janus and the Quirinal of the god Quirinus. Nearly all the early Christian churches were built on, or over, the foundations and ruins of pagan temples, such as the Pantheon, where Victor Emmanuel II, King Umberto I, and Queen Margherita are buried, and daily Masses are said. As in the old days the Romans had their public worships and pagan processions, now they have the processions with the statues of the Blessed Virgin, and some of the saints. One of the delightful sights to be seen in Rome on Saturday afternoon before Easter, are the priests going round their parish, visiting all their parishioners, to bless the houses and the food which is to be eaten on Easter Sunday. The priests walk through the streets attired in a short surplice, generally edged with priceless lace. He has his white stole round his neck and wears his black berretta. He is preceded by two acolytes with cassock and surplice ; one of them carries the holy water in a valuable aspersorium, and the other swings an incensor. In every house, rich and poor, the dining-room table is specially laid for the occasion with the best table-cloth and, for those who possess it, the choicest china, on which is placed all the food, cooked and uncooked, that is to be eaten on Easter Day. Easter Sunday lunch is traditional and is made quite a family affair. No Roman would dare to alter the menu. One starts lunch with hard-boiled eggs, which are painted in all colours, and *salame* (a kind of sausage) and smoked ham; this to be followed by roast lamb (the Easter lamb) and then the Roman *crostata*, which is fruit tart cooked in a special way.

Of course there have been great changes in many social conditions. People who in the days when we lived in Rome, used to shut up their houses for two or three months in the summer, put dust-covers over the furniture, send the silver to the bank, and take an expensive holiday, can no longer afford this.

To-day, owing to better communications and first-class automobile roads—the work of Benito Mussolini—it is possible to reach the sea and country comfortably and in a short time. City clerks in the hot summer months, after a gruelling day at the office, can now pay rush visits to the sea in the evening and enjoy a bathe and the sea air. By using the new Rome–Ostia road, the coast can now be reached in half an hour; and so even those people whose incomes have been sadly reduced, if they are not able to take a long holiday, at least are able to visit the sea and participate in the summer-holiday activities of the nearest resorts.

The other day my friends motored me to Ostia before dinner to see the sunset there. And as I drove along the marvellous *auto strada* (motor road), which at night is lit up all the way from Rome by thousands of powerful electric lamps; which are even brighter than daylight, I could not help remembering the old cobbled country road that it used to be in my young days, when it took three full hours to get there with a carriage and pair!

One lives so much one's daily life in Rome, amongst ancient buildings and antiquities of all sorts, that one almost loses the sense of how ancient they are ; therefore to us Romans it does not seem at all strange that the salt pans founded by Ancus Martius at Ostia twenty-five centuries ago are still in use. It was at this same period that the name of Porta Salaria (Salty Door) was given to the gate of Rome, through which the inhabitants of Sabina used to pass, after having made their purchases of Ostian salt.

The Rome of to-day is a much bigger city than that of three or four decades ago. With the faster pace of modern life, and with the increase of traffic in the capital, Mussolini was faced with the necessity of widening many of the Roman streets. As an indirect result of the widening and pulling-down of old buildings, new Forums have been brought to light, and the city has acquired a new aspect and a new beauty. Appreciation of the antique is inborn in every Roman, whether he be of Royal blood or of the lowliest origin. To-day one still sees people of all ages, many of them hurrying home after their day's work, pause for a few moments to look for the thousandth time at the Foro Argentina, the Forum, or at one of Rome's many other historic monuments. After a few minutes of reverie and peaceful gazing, they then—almost regretfully—remember that they are awaited at home and hasten on.

Mussolini also has recognised that modern life imposes a severe strain especially on city dwellers, and that if their efficiency is to be maintained, their physical and mental conditions must be kept at the highest possible level. Working in an office for eight hours daily, is not conducive to robust health, and if the leisure hours are spent idly in the home, or in the unhealthy atmosphere of the cinemas and theatres, even greater evil is done.

With the object of improving the physique of the nation in general, and of the city worker in particular, the Duce has made exercise and sport practically compulsory for the young; and they have been catered for in Rome on a grand scale. At the foot of the Monte Mario he has constructed the Foro Mussolini, as fine and handsome a stadium as one could wish for, which is equipped with facilities for all kinds of games, gymnastics, and sport. There are opportunities for tennis, archery, throwing the discus, fencing, and swimming, in addition to a magnificent riding-school, among many other things; nothing has been forgotten. The centre arena is surrounded with a series of marble figures, each of which symbolises a particular branch of sport or athletics, many of the figures being reproductions of famous statues in the Roman museums. Also attached to the stadium there is a college in which there are both boarders and day-boys, who receive a training to qualify them to act as instructors of physical culture.

A new and healthier set of youthful citizens is already apparent. Children instead of playing in the streets when school is over, and youths instead of idling in the cafés or at street corners, occupy themselves with properly organised games or athletics. They look healthy; they hold themselves upright; and they have an energy and vitality which the youths of many other cities might well envy.

Competition among them is keen. A new spirit has been' created. Their expression is one of sunshine, active hope, and fulfilment.

Although it was winter, I saw young men of eighteen and twenty years of age, dive into the Tiber and swim from one bank to the other—before making their way to the University.

The houseboats belonging to the Swimming Club are crowded from an early hour in the morning. After their swim, the students have their breakfast and hot coffee and then proceed to their work.

Not least of Mussolini's achievements was the Concordato with the Holy See in 1929. Many articles and books have been written about the political, international and religious aspects of this very important historical event. But what, I think, will interest the reader, is an insight concerning the effect on the Roman soul, the soul of the Roman people, which, on this subject, is completely different from anybody else's in the whole world. For the very good reason that, for centuries, the Roman had united, in *one sole* person, the two supreme authorities which governed him : the temporal, and the spiritual ; and this one person was the Pope. It was a complete dictatorship of the body and soul, for the intrinsic significance of the word " dictator " is one who dictates laws and enforces them. We must remember that Rome was unique in the world in this respect, because other nations and the other Italian towns, though being spiritually under the laws of the Pope, yet for their material and temporal laws and governments they were under their princes and rulers. It is probably this one complete control which made the Roman character so familiar with God and the saints, as I have already mentioned in the course of this book. Therefore, whatever his political opinions might have been, when the Roman found himself suddenly having two distinct kings instead of one, it was like a disintegration of his inner self, and he did not know exactly how, or where to make a separation between the laws and allegiance he owed to his two sovereigns. He loved both ; for the Roman by instinct loves authority and needs to look up to somebody ; but it took each one, individually, years of conflict of their thoughts and feelings before they found their *juste milieu* of spiritual and mental adjustment. They ultimately did so ; but there was always a sore feeling that their two kings should *officially* not be on speaking terms.

Therefore the Concordato was a real *festa* in the heart of every Roman. Finally, there was peace within and without.

Externally, it is true, the Rome of 1937 is very different from the Rome of the days when my father used to lead me by the hand to look at Castel Sant Angelo, where our ancestor had had so much power. But like a beautiful woman whose fashion of dress evolves and changes year by year as the necessities of life demand, Rome in herself is unchangeable. Her heart, her soul, her hopes, her smile of welcome, are even stronger than before ; they are enhanced by her modern activity. Fresh blood flows in her veins ; her heartbeats remain as strong as ever. Rome is truly the Eternal City.

Lightning Source UK Ltd.
Milton Keynes UK
UKHW011444030920
369293UK00001B/399